SOCIOLOGICAL BACKGROUNDS OF ADULT EDUCATION

Papers Presented at a Syracuse University Conference
October, 1963, Sagamore, New York

Edited by HOBERT W. BURNS
Dean, School of Education
Hofstra University

CENTER *for the* **STUDY OF LIBERAL EDUCATION FOR ADULTS**

A Reprint From:

PUBLICATIONS IN CONTINUING EDUCATION

Syracuse University

John E. Corbally, Jr., Chancellor
Alexander N. Charters, Vice President for Continuing Education
Doris S. Chertow, Editor, Publications in Continuing Education

Publications in Continuing Education
105 Roney Lane
Syracuse, New York 13210

March 1970

FOREWORD

The materials incorporated within this volume were originally presented by the authors at a Sagamore conference, organized by University College of Syracuse University in the fall of 1963. This event was the second in a series at which leading social scientists and adult educators were brought together to consider problems of mutual interest and concern. Major papers prepared for the first conference in the series, held in 1962, were published by the Center for the Study of Liberal Education for Adults: Psychological Backgrounds of Adult Education (Notes and Essays No. 40). The present volume continues the process of sharing with a wider audience the ideas which have emerged from these significant conferences.

This year it has been possible to include commentary by adult education practitioners and by sociologists with special concern for the application of research as well as condensed versions of the research summaries which served as basic resource material for the discussions. Many contrasting opinions are expressed, reflecting the diversity of approach which characterizes the adult education movement. Although the topics selected for consideration cover a broad range, no claim is made that they encompass a comprehensive treatment of the subject or that any topic has been dealt with exhaustively. Rather, it is hoped that the reader will be encouraged to pursue his own explorations in the field.

It seems essential to maintain a continuing interchange of ideas between those who undertake basic investigations in the social and behavioral sciences and those who are confronted with the immediate tasks of educational program development. Such a dialogue is mutually beneficial. As a result, procedures may become more effective, and areas of needed research become more clearly identified. The Sagamore conferences have been designed to serve these ends.

Acknowledgment should be given to the work of Dr. Hobert Burns, formerly of Syracuse University, now Dean of the School of Education, Hofstra University, who served as general chairman of the conference and editor of its proceedings. Special thanks are also due to James Whipple, Assistant Director of the Center for the Study of Liberal Education for Adults, whose continuing counsel in relation to this project has been invaluable.

Alexander Charters
Dean
University College,
Syracuse University

May, 1964

INTRODUCTION

While it is true that adult higher education plays an increasingly important role in the great American enterprise of mass education,[1] it is yet but one phase of the complex cultural drama called public higher education. Even so, even though it is but an integral part of the larger educational whole, when viewed as an object of sociological inquiry and analysis adult education is clearly seen to be qualitatively different from either public or higher education in that its structures, functions, purposes, and—above all—clientele are often sui generis.

This difference makes a difference, not only for the adult educator who must design and implement curricula but for the sociologist who would take education as his subject of study. This is not to say that the sociological principles which might be applied to an investigation of adult education are uniquely different from those used in an analysis of, say, medical education or Catholic education; nor is it to say that the sociologist who elects to specialize in education uses different intellectual tools than one who specializes in industrial sociology, medical sociology, or the sociology of work. But it is to say, following Kuhlen,[2] that the sociological backgrounds of adult education differ from those of elementary, secondary, and "normal" higher education not in general principle but in particular data which indicate how the individuals and institutions involved in adult higher education differ uniquely from those involved in other educational activities.

---

1. Cf. Burton Clark, "Knowledge, Industry, and Adult Competence" and John W. C. Johnstone, "Adult Uses of Education: Fact and Forecast," in this volume.

2. Raymond G. Kuhlen, "Psychology and Adult Education: Introductory Comments," Psychological Backgrounds of Adult Education, Chicago: Center for the Study of Liberal Education for Adults, 1963, p. 1, says: "The psychology of adult education differs from the psychology of elementary and secondary education not so much in its principles as in the descriptive data . . ."

The full import of this for adult education may well lie in the fact that programs of adult education are often "tailor made" to meet the demands of clientele groups or, similarly, to prepare clientele groups to meet the demands of a changing society. In this sense, and given its unique purposes, adult education is in a more advantageous position to be responsive to those pertinent sociological data which contain implicit suggestions for programming than are elementary, secondary, or "normal" higher education which are historically less responsive, if often not impervious, to current or anticipated needs in educational programming. Thus, when viewed as an instrument of planning—as it can be with full justification—sociological analysis is of potentially greater value to adult education than to other, more traditional forms of education; and the adult educator has perhaps a greater need to be more sophisticated in awareness and application of sociological data to his enterprise.

The basic purpose of the Conference on Sociological Backgrounds of Adult Education was to "bring together a small and select group of sociologists, of sociologists of education, and adult educators to explore in some depth those sociological materials most relevant to adult education" in the hope that "we may reduce somewhat the gap between the academician and the practitioner."

The Conference was the continuation of a dialogue between social scientists and adult educators[3] inaugurated in 1962 in the expectation not only that practical purposes of adult education might be served but that significant research might be stimulated. To help instrument these expectations the Conference Committee, composed of individuals from the University College of Syracuse University and the Center for the Study of Liberal Education for Adults, identified five areas of inquiry—demography, social change, adult status and roles, adult value changes, and adult uses of education—of interest to adult educators and invited a group of distinguished sociologists to summarize the pertinent research in each area. The papers were not to be focused on practical or programmatic considerations but to fundamental sociological considerations. To provide the bridge between data and practice two respondents—one a sociol-

3. A Conference on Psychological Backgrounds of Adult Education was held at Syracuse University's Sagamore Conference Center, Sagamore, New York, in October, 1962.

ogist of education and the other an adult educator—were invited to criticize the paper and point out new and promising areas of sociological inquiry as well as suggest what each paper might mean by way of practical consideration.

As might be expected there was no one central tendency running through papers and responses such that, in summary, it could fairly be said that the Conference produced consensus on some given set of theorems or programs.

As these papers demonstrate, it is abundantly clear that the sociologist, as sociologist, has no prescriptions to offer the adult educator. He can offer only descriptions—as have Drs. Sheldon, Clark, Havighurst, Friedmann, and Johnstone—which the adult educator can use, in conjunction with psychological data and philosophical position, to create programs of adult education which seem proper and pertinent for specific individuals in specific situations. The strength of adult education may well lie in an assumed weakness: programs of adult education in university colleges, evening programs, extension divisions, and centers for continuing education lack common structure, common function, common purpose. In this diversity may well be found strength rather than weakness for, as the Syracuse University Conference on the Sociological Backgrounds of Education has clearly shown, when brought to bear upon adult education, sociological skills do not necessarily yield data which are unambiguous and point clearly in any one given direction.

Hobart W. Burns
Hofstra University

TABLE OF CONTENTS

KNOWLEDGE, INDUSTRY, AND ADULT COMPETENCE[1]

Burton R. Clark
University of California

Rapidly changing knowledge and technology are among the most critical social facts of our time. Changes in scientific information and in industrial technique bear hard on adult life by increasing the requirements
of personal competence and by extending the problem of human obsolescence. These modern trends also work hardships on the training institutions that prepare the young for adulthood and that provide for the re-
education and continuing education of adults. I would like to inquire into
the impact on society of changes in knowledge and industry, first, to
trace changes taking place in the world of work; second, to specify consequences of these changes for other institutions; and, third, to speak
directly to the problem of personal competence. I will begin by review-
ing the historic shift in industry and occupations and then depict a new
kind of industry—the knowledge industry—that now shapes adult life and
society. The knowledge industry has effects extending in every direction;
and I will concentrate on six important effects of this modern prime-
mover.

Change in Industry and Occupations

The changes that take place in industry and occupations under increasing industrialism are widely known and can be quickly reviewed.
To sense the character of the times it is useful to recall that throughout
the history of man, until the last 50 to 75 years, most human labor in a
society was devoted to the gathering and raising of food. We start with
agriculture as the primary industry when tracing modern changes in the
nature of work. In the agricultural stage work is relatively unskilled, and
for the most part is closely identified with the home. As industrialization

---

1. Some parts of this paper draw heavily upon Burton R. Clark,
Educating the Expert Society, San Francisco: Chandler Publishing Co.,
1962; and "Sociology of Education," in Robert E. L. Faris (ed.), Hand-
book of Sociology, Chicago: Rand McNally and Co., forthcoming.

gets underway in a society, some men move into manufacturing—the turning of resources into products through technical processes. At this early stage of industrialism, work is still manual for the most part and at first there is little rise in skill. The worker has simply taken his hands from the farm to the factory, or from the plow in the field to a room inside his house to work on materials put out to him by an entrepreneur. But as industrialization advances, work changes radically: jobs are separated from the home and grouped in large organizations; those who continue to work with their hands must acquire skills of increasing complexity and requisite training, and there emerges semi-skilled and skilled blue-collar occupations; an increasing proportion of the work becomes mental labor and there emerges a white-collar office force in the factory. Then, as an economy becomes modern, moving into a stage of advanced industrialism, the emphasis shifts from manufacturing toward service or tertiary industry, toward the distribution of products and various forms of service and economic facilitation: transportation, finance, insurance, wholesale and retail trade, government, professional work, domestic labor. Within this large and varied sector work is predominantly mental.

With industrialization, with this shift from agriculture to manufacturing to service industry, society is characterized by an ever growing division of labor. In a pre-literate society, labor may be divided only by sex and age, work for women and work for men, work for the younger male and work for the older man. In a society of early industrialization, characterized by modest complexity, different occupations may number in the several hundred. Great Britain had approximately 430 occupational titles in 1841. In a society of advanced industrialism, the different kinds of jobs number into the thousands; over 25,000 in the United States in 1940.[2] In sum: labor is ever more divided; it shifts constantly from manual to mental, from hand to head work; and there are rising levels of skill required in both the manual and the mental labor.

These basic changes in industry and work are reflected in wholesale changes in the labor force. The proportion of all workers in the United States in agriculture dropped during the nineteenth century from nearly

_____

2. Theodore Caplow, The Sociology of Work. Minneapolis: The University of Minnesota Press, 1954.

2

75 per cent in 1820 to about 50 per cent in 1880 and about 37 per cent in 1900. Farm workers have continued to decline and now form less than 10 per cent of the work force; manual and service workers constituted

TABLE 1

LABOR FORCE, 1900-1959

(In per cent)

Occupational Category	1900	1910	1920	1930	1940	1950	1959
Farm	37.5	30.9	27.0	21.2	17.4	11.8	9.9
Manual and service	44.9	47.7	48.1	49.4	51.5	51.6	48.0
White-collar	17.6	21.3	24.9	29.4	31.1	36.6	42.1
Total	100.0	100.0	100.0	100.0	100.0	100.0	100.0

Source: Fritz Machlup, The Production and Distribution of Knowledge in the United States. Princeton: Princeton University Press, 1962, p. 382.

about 45 per cent of all workers in 1900, rose slightly to a peak of approximately 52 per cent in 1940 and 1950, and now are proportionately in decline. The white-collar category is the great gainer, increasing steadily from 18 per cent of the work force in 1900, to 42 per cent in 1959. These percentages contain very large shifts in numbers, since the labor force grew from 29 million in 1900 to 65 million in 1959; farm workers decreased in number from 11 to 6 million, and were in 1959, 59 per cent of what they were in 1900; manual and service workers increased from 13 to 31 million, an increase of 238 per cent; white-collar men and women increased from 5 to 27 million, or 540 per cent. Since 1940, a twenty-year period, farm workers have decreased 3 million, or by 29 per cent; manual workers have increased 4 million, or by 16 per cent; and white-collar workers have increased by 11 million, or by 69 per cent.[3]

These figures provide the gross picture of change in industry and occupations under industrialization in this country. They form a base from which we can proceed to the fascinating, rapid changes that have

3. Fritz Machlup, The Production and Distribution of Knowledge in the United States. Princeton: Princeton University Press, 1962, pp. 381-82.

been taking place since the end of World War II, changes that have worked to bind education closely to the economy, both as a force upon the economy and as an institution which is asked to adjust its own schedules to economic demands.

The labor force is characterized by growing expertise. Critical in the expanding and intensifying expertness is the rise to great influence of what has been called knowledge-producing workers. Using a generous definition of who produces knowledge—a definition that includes those who disseminate information—Machlup has identified five major knowledge industries: research and development, education, media of communication, information machines (e.g., computers), and information services (e.g., legal advice, accounting and auditing).[4] The knowledge industries, thus defined, expanded from a tenth to nearly a third of the labor force between 1900 and 1959, increasing by 600 per cent in numbers while the labor force as a whole increased by 135 per cent.

The most dynamic element within this broadly defined industry is research and development, the activity centered on the production of socially-new knowledge. Located in industry, governmental agencies, universities, and non-profit organizations (e.g., Rand Corporation, Stanford Research Institute, Arthur D. Little), "R and D" constitutes a massive assault on innovation. It is a commitment of large numbers of scientists and highly trained technologists, organized in laboratories, to the search for new knowledge and technique <u>and</u> to the immediate development of the new for practical use. The increase of men employed in R and D is so large that it is revolutionary. The scientists and engineers working in research and development laboratories approximated 10,000 in 1920, 85,000 in 1941, and 150,000 in 1950; 225,000 in 1954, 325,000 in 1958,[5] and an estimated 425,000 in 1962. This enterprise is now financed at a rate of over 17 billion dollars a year.

R and D is a segment of the economy off which we dare not take our eyes for very long, for in it we have a new economic prime-mover. If captains of industry have long been men of power, and if labor leaders were the new men of power of the 1930's and 1940's, it is the scientists

---

4. Ibid., <u>passim</u>.
5. <u>Ibid</u>., p. 159.

and engineers who are the new men of power of the 1950's and 1960's, at least in the sense that these are the men whose acts affect our lives even where they do not participate in the decisions on the uses of their innovations. To speak of these men is to speak of atomic energy, electronics, information machines, and now the space industry. Let us highlight a few of the many avenues of impact of this numerically small sector of industry upon the rest of society.

The Impact of R and D

Research and development is a producer of new industries. Electronics was perhaps the leading case in point in the 1950's, an industry whose growth was sparked by the invention of the transistor in the Bell Laboratories in 1948. Apparently space technology will be an even more important example in the 1960's. The new industries thus created grow very rapidly and become pace-setters in the economy and determiners of the general economic health of the nation.

Research and development dictates that the newer forms of major industry must be located where there is a scientific-educational base. Because of this, the economic well-being of cities and whole regions of the country is at stake. Between the Korean War and 1961, defense contracts awarded by the U.S. Department of Defense shifted sharply, with the East North Central states the great losers (down from 27.4 per cent to 11.8 per cent) and the Pacific and Mountain states the great gainers (up from 18.6 per cent to 32.6 per cent).[6] The geographic shift in procurement followed changes in weapons systems; the military moved from production line items, such as tanks and rifles, to missiles and electronic equipment. As put in a Defense Department report: "the more recent emphasis has been upon research and development, and upon fewer, far more costly, weapon units. Traditional metal fabricating processes are giving way to more intricate and sophisticated techniques. In consequence, blue-collar workers are fewer, while scientists, engineers and technicians multiply in establishments serving defense procurement needs."[7]

Increasingly, the large contracts for weapons production go to those

---

6. Office of the Secretary of Defense, "The Changing Patterns of Defense Procurement," 1962, pp. 3-4.

7. Ibid., p. 2.

who received research and development awards. In defending the fact that the basic research contracts have been concentrated in a few states, particularly California and Massachusetts, the Defense Department has pointed to the importance of going to where the competence is.

"Defense must seek its needs where capability exists." The Department concluded: "Defense policy stresses awards on merit. Local initiative seeking defense business must direct itself to the creation of capability responsive to the exacting needs of modern warfare. Communities which fail to recognize this fact, and which fail to energize and mobilize their institutions to adjust to it, cannot reasonably anticipate a major role in future defense procurement."[8]

The Defense Department was able to claim that it was simply acting as intelligent management everywhere is now acting, and quoted from a brochure put out by a newly established research center in Texas:

"Management planners, in considering sites for new or expanded facilities, have found that the availability of trained minds overshadows even such factors as the labor market, water supply, and power sources. The evidence is overwhelming: Route 128 encircling Boston, the industrial complex around San Francisco Bay, that related to the California Institute of Technology and UCLA in the Los Angeles area, and other similar situations are cogent examples of the clustering of industry around centers of learning. Such a migration arises from the need by industry for access to persons with advanced training who can translate the new science into vastly improved or wholly new products."[9]

Thus, research and development enters sharply into the geographic location of industry; into the economic health of cities and states, with that health particularly dependent on the presence of universities; and into the geographic movement of workers, particularly the technologist.

Research and development is a commitment to an acceleration of change in technology and industry. With the great growth of R and D, the creation of knowledge is now extensively and intensively institutionalized. It is less left to chance, it is less a by-product of other functions, such as cultural transmission. The conservation of knowledge has led in mod-

---

8. Ibid., p. 11.

9. Ibid., p. 10, quoting from brochure entitled, "Charter of Progress," Graduate Research Center of the Southwest, Dallas, Texas.

est degree to the development of knowledge. In modern times, the point is, many more men spend much more time than ever before in the deliberate development of knowledge. We now have differentiated, specialized, full-time concentration on the production and utilization of knowledge. Technical invention is transformed from amateur tinkering to systematic inquiry and development based on expanding scientific theory. The pre-World War II world knew nothing like the current and ever-expanding commitment to research. The specialization, the division of labor, the magnitude of the commitment of resources, all are unprecedented. The winning of top honors in science is somewhat rationalized, made predictable, since the "big successes" increasingly come from having at hand a major laboratory with precious equipment, large staff, and much money. The production of a steady stream of inventions is also rationalized and predictable in the large industrial laboratories. When we institutionalize research in such massive concentrations, we apparently commit ourselves to an accelerating pace of change.

Research and development has a heavy impact on other institutions. Education, for one, is very much affected. Higher education is deeply involved in R and D, partly as a location for much scientific and technological work and especially as the agency that trains the scientists and engineers who man the laboratories wherever they are located. Higher education has a monopoly as supplier of scientists and engineers, and the growth of R and D makes very great demands on higher education for an increased supply of such highly trained men.

R and D is the extreme case of a general phenomenon: brain workers of an ever-higher calibre are the economic need of societies in advanced stages of industrialism. These workers must have education; educational institutions have the awesome responsibility of selecting and training this special kind of worker. This responsibility is now one of the critical links of education to the economy, and puts education into a special dynamic relationship to the economy, one where it can retard or accelerate technological advance. A constricted output of technologists reduces the amount of effort sustained in research and development; an enlarged flow of highly trained men into this unusual sector of the economy, on the other hand, makes possible a large and varied and expanding R and D establishment, and may accelerate the growth of the economy. The technologists prepared by education go into an industry that both creates new knowledge and puts it to work. We may hypothesize that this industry is more subject to a principle of acceleration and multiplier effects than previous forms of industry. The new knowledge is made the base for new technologies which lead to new industries and to the revamping of some existing industries.

In short, higher education has a particularly dynamic impact on the economy in the determination of the supply of people with advanced education, especially scientists and engineers, for this supply enters increasingly to determine the pace of economic growth. With this, we must note and emphasize, the possibility emerges that education cannot overtrain and overproduce for the economy—an historic concern here but particularly in other countries. For if increased supply of high competence means more and varied innovation leading to economic growth, then a rising supply constantly accelerates the demand for trained personnel. The greater the present supply of such people, the greater the future demand for them. Thus, there is no simple relationship of fixed economic demand for competence and a definite educational response to it. Supply interacts to determine demand.

In 1962, a committee of the Organization for Economic Co-operation and Development came to this country to study scientific manpower and higher education and to make recommendations. In its report to the O.E.C.D., the committee concluded:

"It may be claimed that demand for people with higher education should not be derived from a predetermined estimate of the development of the economy. On the contrary, it is the supply of such personnel that, in combination with other factors, determines the pace of economic growth. Educational targets, thus, should be regarded as one facet of general growth targets."[10]

If the impact of research and development is heavy in the case of education, so it is with many other institutions. The military establishment, for example, is altered throughout its length and breadth. The new technology produced by R and D is the primary force in modern times for changing the military. The new weapons systems demand different skills on the part of military personnel; hence, the military now needs a differ-

---

10. "Scientific Manpower and Higher Education in U.S.A." O.E.D.C. Country Review of the United States, 1963.

ent kind of labor force. The modern military man increasingly emerges as a technologist; there is specialization all down the line. Higher levels of skill are required, and the skills are similar to civilian skills: "engineers, machine maintenance specialists, health service experts, logistic and personnel technicians. The concentration of personnel with 'purely' military occupational specialties has fallen from 93.2 per cent in the Civil War to 28.8 in the post-Korean Army, and to even lower percentages in the Navy and Air Force."[11] The military thus no longer consists of a mass of unskilled men.

The fundamental change taking place in the nature of military work alters even the rank and authority structures. The hierarchy becomes less of a pyramid as technologists are added at the middle and upper levels of the enlisted and officer ranks. Along with the officer of combat vigor who fills the role of heroic leader of the troops, we have increasing numbers of officer technologists who provide technical expertise, and military managers whose role it is to coordinate an increasingly complex organization staffed with a growing array of specialists. Much attention goes to lateral coordination of groups of experts, rather than to rigid discipline and direct command. The problems of authority thus produced are acute; it is difficult for many of the old warriors to adjust to the presence and the competence of the technologist and the manager. As elsewhere in society, there is in the military an expertizing of work, and all features of military organization are under pressure to adapt to this fundamental trend.

Modern technological advance, largely a result of research and development, makes the unskilled man unemployable. His unemployability is a relatively new phenomenon in human history, one linked to the rising curves of skill and knowledge. Always before, the unskilled man constituted cheap labor. But now the productivity of the educated man is expanded many fold by the technology at his command, and the gap between the productivity of the skilled and unskilled is widening to the point where the unskilled are driven from work. The unskilled are no longer cheap labor, especially since ideals of social justice, e.g., minimum wage, will not permit their wages to shrink ever lower to compensate for their ever lower (relative) productivity. It is economically efficient to mechanize

---

11. Morris Janowitz, The Professional Soldier. New York: The Free Press of Glencoe, 1960, p. 9.

the unskilled work in ever more fields and to retire the low-skill positions from the occupational structure.

The wiping out of jobs at the lower levels of skills, an irreversible process in the technological society, bears hard on education. If education possibly cannot overtrain for an expanding, job-upgrading economy, it can certainly undertrain and with results that are increasingly disastrous for the individual and malintegrative for society. The young with little education and no skill have no place to go. The problem of school dropouts is their impact on the labor market. The jobs they used to go to are no longer there. At the same time, in the face of higher retention rates by the schools, there is a much larger number of dropouts, because of high birthrate. We are witnessing a race between the rising educational requirements for jobs and the rising educational attainments of youth. The requirements appear at this time to be outrunning the attainments for an increasing proportion as well as absolute number of youth—at least a jobless rate of 16 per cent among teenage workers this past year would lead us to think so.

The interaction of change in knowledge and change in technique that is epitomized by R and D causes a rapid obsolescence of skill, necessitating more retraining at all levels of skill. Blue-collar workers need retraining for different occupations as machines and new processes replace them in their original line of work; a new pipeline carrying coal in a liquid stream may require only five men trained in handling computer controls, in place of 1,200 railroad men whose jobs were dependent on the coal traffic. With the rapid growth of engineering knowledge, the engineer of ten years experience who has not engaged in substantial re-education is very likely to have less competence and value than a new engineering graduate. Hence engineers are faced with the need to go back to the classroom or have the classroom brought to them in industry if they are to maintain competence. Teachers at all levels of education face a growing need for periodic retraining; engineering faculties are already grappling with this problem.

The accelerating obsolescence of skill and knowledge is a pressure to extend education over the adult years of work; it is a pressure to diversify education in such forms as the governmental manpower training program; it is a pressure to move educational work into such locations as the work shop and the union hall. We may expect all institutions of work to become institutions of training in larger degree. The retraining and reorienting of adults apparently must become a major educational mission as societies move deeper into the modern technological stage.

To review: a century of industrialization has seen great change in the nature of work and in the definitions of adult competence. In the advanced industrialism characteristic of the United States since 1945, change in work is accelerating, due to the dynamic element introduced into the economy by a massive commitment to scientific and technological innovation. Expanding and important occupational groups have specialized skills based on expanding bodies of knowledge. The most important of these groups in influence on the economy and society are scientists and engineers, for it is their work that produces the rising curve of technology that transforms other men's work, renders other men's jobs obsolete, and renders other men themselves obsolete. Many of our present occupations are headed for oblivion; and we face the possibility that the transistor shall inherit the earth.

The Problem of Adult Competence

Thus, as we look at modern knowledge, occupations, and industry, and at the swiftness of evolution in technical and social affairs, we sense that adult competence is a very problematic thing. The total balance of effects of modern trends in creating and destroying jobs is unclear. It may well be that more jobs are created than are destroyed, but they are very different kinds of jobs. And what is clear is that individuals are sharply affected and have good reason to fear technological change. Jobs destroyed in an industry are not necessarily replaced in that industry, or in that sector of the economy, or in that part of the country. Or, if they are, they likely call for new skills. This situation is not entirely new; under advancing industrialism, men have always had to change jobs during their lifetime. But it is the extensiveness and especially the rapidity of the change that makes such a difference. Positions are retired or revamped at a more rapid rate, and for more workers. This greatly extends the problem of personal skill and worth, the problem of having competence for a life-time of work. It greatly extends the problem of the meaning of work, what part work plays in a man's sense of his place in the world, his function, his reason for existence.

We spoke earlier of the obsolescence of an engineer's knowledge and

11

skill. While this is a meaningful problem, it is a relatively minor problem for society and for the individuals concerned, compared with situations at lower levels of skill where men sense the possibility of abolition of their jobs over-night and wholesale, and where other men have no potential for work because they have no employable skills. We do not have major social conflicts brewing over the obsolescence of engineers' knowledge. Engineers make out; at worst, they become salesmen, or become liaison representatives to a supplier or distributor, or become managers, or join the Peace Corps. We do have major conflict brewing over obsolescence at the lower levels, where a whole job classification can be phased out, and we do have social dynamite in unemployment, especially in the case of Negro youth, where lack of job skill is compounded by and interacts with discrimination in training and in employment.

We also face a growing possibility that many men who nominally are at work are actually engaged in useless work and in unwork.[12] When men must choose between no job and a job that is make-work, it is clear they will choose the make-work; and when men anticipate that they are likely to have to face this choice, they build the make-work into their occupations. Such proud and elite craftsmen as the printers refuse to wipe such practices off the books, even when the practice disgusts them. The fear that the machine is going to threaten one's job, certainly a harsh effect of rapid technological change, is a fear that instead of affecting several occupations may now or soon be affecting the lower half to two-thirds of the work force.

One general response to the problem of adult competence thus raised in modern times is massive investment in education and retraining. It is now clear that in the 60's and 70's we shall see a proliferating and diffuse enterprise devoted to the task of appropriate preparation and retraining for work, and perhaps even appropriate adjustment for non-work. This means more schooling located within industry, with industry taking a public responsibility; it means more adult-level schooling programs supported by government independent of present schools and colleges.

What does it mean for the secondary school and the college? The schools and colleges are torn in two directions: one toward specific job

---

12. Paul Jacobs, "Dead Horse and the Featherbird." Santa Barbara, California: Center for the Study of Democratic Institutions, 1962.

preparation, in order to give the young initial competence, and the other toward a general preparation, in order to give the young the potential for later re-education and re-adjustment. Several leading social scientists have speculated that the great need is the second, that the school must somehow learn to educate for greater adaptability. Karl Mannheim has maintained that the school of the past was "a training ground for imitative adjustment to an established society," while the school of today is (or ought to be) "an introduction into an already dynamic society."[13] In this view, the rapidity of social change in our time means that appropriate behavior in the next generation will differ extensively from the ways of the past; hence, to instill only traditional forms of culture in the schools is potentially malintegrative. No one knows ahead of time, however, what will be the functional behavior patterns of the future. The answer, then, is to educate for adaptability, i.e., educate the young to be perceptive and understanding of the social environment and flexible and imaginative in dealing with it, with little control by the patterns of the past.

Margaret Mead has speculated along somewhat similar lines while worrying about the competence of school teachers. She maintains that for the teacher "age and experience become not orienting factors but disorienting ones, so that the teacher of 20 years' experience may face her class less confidently than the teacher with only two."[14] The young early incorporate into their thinking, especially from exposure to the mass media, new ideas that many older persons will never fully assimilate. Mead has advocated wholesale periodic re-orientation of teachers, including orientation excursions to the playground and the nursery school as well as to the home, to acquaint the teacher with the new perspectives, interests, and activities of the young. No one knows, however, if older teachers are sufficiently flexible to undergo periodic reorientation, and the nature of their initial training may be critical in establishing a potential adjustability.

In societies of old, age and experience generally brought to a man superior cultural comprehension and associated prestige. Modern society

---

13. Karl Mannheim, Freedom, Power, and Democratic Planning. London: Routledge and Kegan Paul, 1951, p. 248.

14. Margaret Mead, The School in American Culture. Cambridge: Harvard University Press, 1951, p. 33.

with its rapid change offers the possibility for us all that age and experience will be disorienting. Unless, that is, people are adaptable enough to be born again, socially and culturally, adaptable enough to change jobs, to move to another part of the country, and—more radical—change their styles of thinking and living. Educating for ever-rising levels of versatility and retrainability has thus emerged as one of the most important educational and social challenges of the time. Unfortunately, the problem is extremely complicated. We now know from a half century of experience with mass education at the elementary and secondary levels that when we move from transmission of a definite body of knowledge to more open, pluralistic, future-oriented forms of educational preparation, we open up a Pandora's box of risks. The criteria of what shall be taught and learned become more ambiguous, leading perhaps to a weaker transmission of the cultural heritage and perhaps then to cultural discontinuity and to slippage in age-old ideals. There is likely to be a general weakening of standards of conduct. Men may be educated to adjust easily and passively to group and organizational demands. Education for flexible man, Mannheim foresaw, is likely to lead to confusion, and may lead to chaos, "the arch-enemy of Democracy."[15] Thus the preparatory agencies of society must avoid extreme individualism as well as cultural orthodoxy. The integration of society is dependent on the capacity of education to blend together an anticipation of a changing future with imitation of the past.

What is the minimal response of society to the problem of adult competence that will get by in the decades ahead? At a minimum, the future adult, sometime in his first 20 years, must receive sufficient basic education that he can later qualify for re-education and re-training. Men must be brought up to and kept ahead of the rising threshold of functional literacy. The new government job retraining programs have come up against a stark fact in the early 60's: men who need retraining the most are likely to get it the least because they cannot qualify for it. They simply do not have the basic education to qualify for relatively simple classes. We can state therefore a new expectation we must hold for the institutions that prepare the young for adulthood: when the young person leaves school, he must have received a basic education to a point that

---

15. Mannheim, op. cit., p. 243.

articulates with the requirements for entering the programs that will train and retrain him as an adult.

What can we ask of society as a maximal response to this problem of adult competence? We can ask that society rapidly assimilate the following two beliefs and make them part of the conventional wisdom. Belief #1: education is more important than work experience. In the past, experience generally increased one's expertise and value. Now we must understand that by itself experience increasingly leads to loss of expertise and value. The value of experience in a job is going down, the value of educational preparation, general and specific, is going up. There is no reason to expect this trend to reverse itself; rather, it will probably accelerate. This is a reversal of the relative value of experience and education in the past, and the conventional wisdom of modern man on this matter needs to be rapidly reversed.

Belief #2: schooling is a normal part of adult life. Military officers in the United States now know that they will spend a large proportion of their career—perhaps a third—going to school.[16] Civilians will increasingly have similar expectation. The work-school pattern can take widely varying forms: part of each day, or each week, or each month, or each year in the classroom in the factory; or, major leaves of absence from work to return to the major training institutions. We already have some industries such as electronics subsidizing their employees in study toward advanced degrees. The U.S. Civil Service has also recently moved in this direction. This pattern needs to be widely understood as part of the wave of the future, and incorporated rapidly into the common understanding.

There is no turning back from this problem of competence. The character of modern knowledge and industry, and particularly the close fusion of the development of knowledge with the development of industry in research and development facilities, dictates that adult life will be characterized by ever sharper requirements of occupational, social, and cultural competence, by deeper problems for the individual of obsolescence and disorientation. In their bearing on adult life, knowledge and industry in the last few years have at last brought us to the point where

---

16. Janowitz, op. cit.

the old expressions of "life-long learning" and "continuing education" become meaningful descriptions of what is required of man. Ours is an educative society and we are undoubtedly on the threshold of an age of adult education.

CHANGING STATUS AND ROLES DURING THE ADULT
LIFE CYCLE: SIGNIFICANCE FOR
ADULT EDUCATION

Robert J. Havighurst
The University of Chicago

The most profound educational change of this century is a change of attitude which no longer regards education as essentially <u>preparatory</u> but regards education as essentially a way of meeting the <u>demands and aspirations of the present period of one's life</u>.

This means that education has uses in every stage of the life cycle; not merely in the stages of childhood and adolescence. Every stage of life in modern society requires a person to learn new things if he is to live up to his own aspirations and the expectations that others have of him.

That is why there is so much emphasis now on educating the mind as an <u>instrument of learning</u> rather than a <u>storehouse of knowledge</u>. That is why so much of the new methods in the schools concentrate on self-initiated learning, on methods of inquiry, use of the library, etc. If the school can educate the child for self-initiated learning, the child will go on learning as an adult.

There are two <u>basic aspects of education</u>, both of which are essential for lifelong learning. They are the <u>instrumental</u> and the <u>expressive</u>. Instrumental education means education for a goal which lies outside and beyond the act of education. In this form, education is an instrument for changing the learner's situation. For example, the learner studies arithmetic so as to be able to exchange money and to buy and sell things and to become a competent scientist or teacher. Or the learner as a young adult studies in his vocational field so as to get a promotion, or studies cooking so as to become a better housewife. Instrumental education is thus a kind of investment of time and energy in the expectation of future gain.

17

Expressive education means education for a goal which lies within the act of learning, or is so closely related to it that the act of learning appears to be the goal. For example, the learner studies arithmetic for the pleasure of learning about numbers and quantities. The learning of arithmetic is its own reward. Or the learner as a young adult studies the latest dances so as to enjoy the dances he and his friends go to. He learns to dance "for fun" and not to become a teacher of dancing, or even to make new friends. Expressive education is a kind of consumption of time and energy for present gain.

In a changing society a competent person needs to make a combination of instrumental and expressive learning at every stage of his life.[*]

He cannot confine learning to one or two stages of his life. Not long ago it was customary to divide the life cycle with a period of infancy and childhood for play, of childhood and adolescence for study, of adulthood for work, and old age for play again. Today nobody can live that way and be a competent member of contemporary society. Rather, the life cycle should be conceived as a rope with parallel strands of play, study, and work each extending all the way through life, but with the work strand having greater thickness in adulthood, while the study and play strands have greater thickness in childhood and adolescence.

Roles and Developmental Tasks of the Adult Life Cycle

The adult educator can usefully see the adult part of the life cycle as consisting of a set of stages or phases which make different demands on education and offer different opportunities to the educator. This is a commonplace observation with respect to children and adolescents. Everybody knows that their educational needs and capabilities change as they grow and develop. Adulthood is much longer, and has fully as much growth and development as the earlier periods.

---

[*]The distinction between instrumental and expressive aspects of education should not be carried too far. There is some intrinsic enjoyment in almost every instrumental form of education, at least if the learner is reasonably successful; and there is some instrumental or extrinsic outcome from almost every expressive form of education. It might be more useful to assign weights between one and 100 to the instrumental and the expressive aspect of any form of education, with the total of the two weights being 100. Then one would need to recognize that a given educational experience would have different pairs of weights for each individual participant.

Two ways of thinking about development during adulthood seem promising. One is to think of the developmental tasks of this segment of life. A developmental task is a task which must be achieved at or about a certain phase in life, if a person is to be judged and to judge himself as a competent person. Failure in a developmental task is likely to be followed by failure in later tasks. Success prepares a person for successful performance of later tasks.

A developmental task is set by three forces: the force of biological development; the force of social demands and expectations; and the force of personal ambition and aspiration. In early childhood the biological and the social forces dominate, while the balance shifts later on, so that in adulthood the social demands and personal aspirations dominate in setting and defining developmental tasks, with the biological changes of middle age and later maturity probably asserting a major force in the years after about 50.

The other way of thinking about development during adulthood is to conceive of adult life as consisting of a set of changing social roles. A social role is a complex of behavior appropriate to a given position in social life, defined by the expectations of society and of the individual. For example, a person in the social role of a father is expected to behave in certain ways as his children grow up, and he learns to expect this behavior of himself. The social expectation and the self-expectation may be more or less equal; a person who is seen as a competent father by other people and who feels himself to be a competent father has a self-expectation which is closely akin to the social expectation concerning a good father.

The common social roles of interest to adult educators are:

> Worker
> Parent
> Spouse
> Home-maker
> Citizen
> Neighbor
> Friend
> Club or association member
> Church member

Each of these social roles can be defined for young adults, middle-aged adults, and older adults, and educational programs can be conceived to help people improve their performance of these roles.[5][6]

Returning to the use of the developmental task concept, it is worth-

19

while to group the tasks of adulthood into two categories which differ in the degree to which they require an <u>instrumental</u> kind of education for successful achievement.

A. Developmental tasks most closely related to instrumental forms of education:

> Preparing for an occupation
> Becoming a competent and responsible worker
> Rearing children
> Setting adolescent children free
> Making a comfortable home
> Becoming an informed and responsible citizen
> Adjusting to bodily changes

B. Developmental tasks for which instrumental forms of education have relatively little value:

> Becoming a member of a friendship group
> Achieving intimate and mutually supportive relations with close friends
> Choosing a marriage partner
> Living intimately with one's spouse
> Becoming a competent church member
> Becoming a club or association member

Education during the adult period is practically essential for competent performance of all the developmental tasks of group A. In following an occupation through a period of 40 years in the modern world, there is no one who can say that he has had to learn nothing new since he commenced his job. Even to keep up with his job generally requires learning new information and skills; while to gain promotion a person generally has to study quite seriously or at least to learn a great deal informally. The coming of automation is actually throwing millions of people out of their jobs and requiring them to learn new ones, either on the job or by taking new training. For many women, entering into the labor force after they have raised their children is a rational and desirable step, but this usually requires specific preparation after the age of 40 or 45.

Furthermore, the task of rearing children has given rise to one of the most popular forms of adult education—courses in child development and family life. Home-making involves learning to cook, to select furniture, to maintain a house and to make a home physically attractive and comfortable, something which men as well as women often study explicitly.

The task of becoming a responsible and informed citizen is likely to be postponed by many people until they reach middle age, when they have

20

achieved their earlier more personal tasks and have time and energy and commitments to their community which induce them to become active citizens.

The physiological and anatomical changes in women and men after about 45 require major adjustments in diet, physical exercise, and work habits that in turn require conscious and explicit attention and consultation with experts. Books and articles are written and read on this subject, which is becoming more and more recognized as an area for education.

In contrast to group A, the achievement of developmental tasks of group B cannot usually be aided by specific instrumental educational activities. Formal education has very little bearing on these tasks. However, some of the expressive forms of education take place in social groups, including the family, clubs, churches, and informal social cliques, and may be of some assistance with such tasks as those of becoming a member of a friendship group, and becoming a competent church or club member.

There is now arising a new developmental task which hardly existed at the beginning of the century—that of making a wise and satisfying use of leisure time. The facts about the increase of available time that is not used up in work or activities related to work are well known. The average individual now has many more hours of free time at his disposal than he had 60 or even 20 years ago. This presents a challenge to the individual—to find constructive ways of passing the time. During the latter years of his life, the psychologist Thorndike spent a good deal of time studying the leisure activities of people. He came to the conclusion that the quality of a society could be measured by the quality of the leisure activities of that society. And when he collected data on the leisure activities of his fellow Americans—watching sports, listening to radio, aimless riding around in automobiles, visiting and drinking—he was pessimistic about the quality of the present North American society.[11]

For all that, the educational use of leisure time is expanding in quantity, and to some extent in quality.

To perform adult roles competently in the midst of rapid social change requires that a person study his way through adulthood. To rely upon what one has learned in school or even in college is completely unsatisfactory. It can only lead to a life of repetition and of stagnation. While repetition is not bad in itself, and indeed may be quite pleasurable under social conditions where it promotes competence, the social changes of the present century make repetition unsuccessful, especially in that part of the society that works with its brains.

The Adult Approach to Education

Adult roles and developmental tasks require adults to view education in certain ways.

Education Is Necessary for Competence in the Area of Work. Whatever the occupation, education is now seen as necessary for minimum competence, and more specialized education as necessary for positions of responsibility. Thus, a company employing young men as future executives may offer to pay their tuition for further education as a means of improving their performance.

The society in general may offer free fundamental education to illiterates so that they can qualify for employment in modern industry. Recently, in Chicago, the Public Welfare Administration required illiterates on relief to attend classes for literacy. This was a venture into compulsory education for adults which was viewed with some misgiving by people who felt that the compulsory element had no place in adult education. But the experiment proved to be successful with some of the welfare clients. They learned to read, and some of them got jobs. This caused some people to think again about the principle of compulsory education. Perhaps it has a place in adult education if that education proves to be instrumental in getting a job for a person who is faced otherwise with chronic unemployment.

Education as a Means of Maintaining Engagement with Society. It is possible to generalize this instrumental view of adult education by noting that in a rapidly changing society education is a means of maintaining active and effective engagement with society. It is the only reliable avenue to success in the roles of worker and citizen. Other avenues have become less reliable.

In a simpler society good moral habits such as honesty, thrift, and responsibility serve to keep a person actively and effectively engaged in the operations of his social environment. Another instrument is the possession of property, with the power and responsibility this entails. But

22

neither good moral habits nor property are enough to guarantee effective engagement in a modern, changing society.

The person who does not keep up with society or keep in with society through continual education is in danger of becoming alienated from society today. Even though his intentions are good, he may lose the ability to interact effectively with his social environment, and then gradually find that the bonds are loosening that keep him engaged in society. Thus failure to take part in adult education may be a forerunner of anomie, or normlessness.

How Socio-Economic Status Affects Participation in Adult Education. The discussion thus far suffers from the narrowness that comes from looking principally at the middle-class aspect of society. What has been said thus far applies mainly to some 40 per cent of the members of a modern industrial society, who can be called "middle class" in their occupations and attitudes. Middle-class people generally regard education as instrumental. They make up a vast majority of those who pursue education as adults. Their jobs require continual education. They tend to raise their children, to look after their business and to conduct themselves as citizens with the aid of reading, study, and formal and informal education.

There are some working-class people who have middle-class attitudes and practices with respect to education. Especially in the field of work they must keep on learning in order to keep on earning, and they know it. On the other hand, there are some middle-class people who cease to learn as soon as possible.

With these exceptions, the generalization stands that adult education today is mainly a middle-class operation. Working-class people generally are more traditional, less given to conscious adjustment to social change, and less likely to engage in self-initiated study. They are less engaged than middle-class people in the workings of the modern society. Spokesmen for the working class, such as Frank Riessman and S. M. Miller,[9] as well as people who are critical of working-class political activity and attitudes, such as S. M. Lipset,[8] tend to agree in seeing the working class as anti-intellectual and unlikely to see adult education as useful to them.

But the growth in relative size of the middle classes in modern so-

23

ciety is bringing more people into adult education. At the same time there are certain working-class groups and movements that have an instrumental or middle-class educational program. Some of the labor unions have this approach.

Education as a Means of Expression. Expressive education is definitely subordinated to instrumental education in the adult field, but not inevitably so. With growing amounts of leisure and with growing experience and possibly with improving taste in the pursuit of leisure activities, it may come about that expressive aspects of adult education will make a relative gain over instrumental aspects.

Such activities are growing in the forms of play-reading in groups, painting, dancing, music making, bridge playing, photography classes, classes in interior decorating, and garden clubs.

Perhaps we see here a working-out in the United States of the choice which every society makes between expressive enjoyment and instrumental improvement. Our choice has been for instrumental improvement in the twentieth as well as the nineteenth century, but it may be shifting.

Dominant Concerns and Adult Education

In thinking about adult education related to the roles and developmental tasks of the adult life cycle it is useful to consider adult life by decades, and to ask about the dominant concerns for each decade. These dominant concerns may suggest a sequence of major topics or centers of emphasis for a program of adult education.

There are various formulations of dominant concerns or predominant developmental tasks. One of the more suggestive ones is that of Erickson[3] who gave the following series of "psychological tasks."

The achievement of identity—personal and occupational identities. A task of adolescence, sometimes continued into the 20's.

The achievement of intimacy—learning to share life intimately with a partner of the opposite sex. A task of early adulthood, generally achieved in the 20's and 30's.

The achievement of generativity—giving the best of oneself to continue and improve human life and human society. Generally achieved in the 40's and 50's.

24

The achievement of integrity—accepting one's life as worthwhile and as something one can take pride in. Generally achieved in the 60's and 70's.

Charlotte Buhler[1] has described the entire life cycle in terms of ten stages, each with a particular problem and a particular achievement.

There is no "correct" number of stages of life and there are no scientifically established age limits for the various stages. The concept of stages or phases is not so exact as this. It is a useful concept when used with some freedom to enable a writer to express ideas about such practical matters as education and guidance.

This essay presents a somewhat different formulation of the stages of the life cycle, which may be useful for those who are interested in understanding the adult part of life, and in developing programs of adult education and guidance.

This scheme uses the concept of a series of dominant concerns, each of which governs the behavior of a person (more or less consciously) during a certain stage of his life. He grows from one dominant concern to the next, and on through eight of them, one for each decade of life.

These concerns, with their characteristic age-periods of dominance, are as follows:

Decade		
0-10	1.	Coming into independent existence
10-20	2.	Becoming a person in one's life
20-30	3.	Focussing one's life
30-40	4.	Collecting one's energies
40-50	5.	Exerting and asserting oneself
50-60	6.	Maintaining position and changing roles
60-70	7.	Deciding whether to disengage and how
70-80	8.	Making the most of disengagement

The timing of these concerns varies with the social group in which one lives. This particular list is essentially descriptive of North American middle-class people. It does not apply to people outside the main stream of social life. Thus it hardly applies to a girl born into a slum-dwelling family who leaves school at the age 15 to get married, has five children by two husbands before she is 30, and spends the rest of her life baby-sitting or working at unskilled jobs until she tires out and dies in her early 60's. Such schemes as this one never apply with much usefulness to people who are anomic and marginal to the society, and there may be a considerable number of such people (as many as 10 or 15 per cent) in a modern industrial society.

Stable working-class people are likely to go through these stages more rapidly than middle-class people, up to the last one, but they do experience the same sequence of dominant concerns.

Women differ slightly from men as far as the timing goes, especially in stages five and six; and women differ substantially from men in the way they deal with these concerns.

This list of exceptions to the generalization implicit in the notion of dominant concerns by decades of life should be supplemented by pointing out the enormous variability of individuals in any ten-year age cohort of people. One person at age 45 will be like a typical 35-year-old while another will be like a typical 55-year-old.

Sources of Dominant Concerns

A dominant concern is the result of the interaction of a developing human organism with the ego in a specific situation. The individual, at a given point of physical and mental maturation, expects himself and is expected by the social group or groups in which he lives to behave in a certain manner, and his physical condition helps to determine what these expectations will be.

As we shall see, the dominant concerns are seen more clearly in the adult decades than they are in childhood and adolescence. This is not due to any absence of dominant concerns in the early part of life, but to just the opposite fact of the presence of several concerns which operate simultaneously. The child and the adolescent have so much to accomplish and such varied tasks to perform that it is difficult to find a single term to include all of the major concerns of these years.

Focussing One's Life. Age 20-30

After the achievement of a <u>psychological</u> identity, there comes a period during which the young adult makes the choices which give him a <u>social</u> identity. Out of a variety of possibilities he selects a particular combination which mark him as a unique person. He takes one job and starts to grow with it. He accepts one marriage partner. He lives in one community. He forms one internally consistent ideology. This is the period of maximum concern with oneself and one's immediate, personal

26

life. Incidentally, it is the age period of least frequency of voting.

A good many young people take the whole decade to accomplish this task of focussing their lives. They experiment with a variety of occupations. They have several love affairs. They try out several religious variants and several political ideologies. The average upper middle-class youth is likely to spend a great deal of time and energy on this concern and is not quite certain, even at the age of 30, that he has achieved a stable focus. On the other hand, there are many young people with simpler identities who achieve a stable focus very early in the twenties or even earlier.

Young women who do not marry are likely to spend a great deal of time and energy trying out one or another possible element of social identity, and to have a complicated, challenging, and sometimes anxious life during this period.

Most young people who are or aspire to be in middle-class occupations use education as an instrument for occupational advancement. They go to college and to graduate school. They take courses at night if they are employed. Education of a more informal kind is used by women as a means of becoming better housekeepers and better mothers.

Collecting One's Energies. Age 30-40

Once the concern for focussing one's life is satisfied, there follows a rather stable and on the whole satisfactory period of collecting one's life resources. As a worker, a person grows in skill and experience, and is promoted accordingly. The young scientist starts to produce research papers. The teacher organizes his material for maximum effectiveness. The mother has her children and rears them with relative ease and pleasure. The homemaker acquires skills and furniture and equipment for the home. The skilled worker reaches the height of his skill and earning power.

This is the period of least introspection or self-awareness. Doubts about oneself have been put to rest. The ego is in command, maturation introduces no new factors, and the situation is generally stable and satisfactory.

Such personality studies as we have of adults in this decade of life indicate that this is a period of relatively great stability, freedom from anxiety, and general psychological well-being. Older women especially are likely to look back upon this decade as the best of their lives.

The studies of adult education students and their choice of courses indicate that education is used as a means of collecting and organizing one's resources during this and the preceding period. Thus the instrumental forms of education predominate, with emphasis on improving occupational and homemaking competence.

However, the expressive forms of education make their appearance, generally around the tasks of becoming a member of a friendship group or a congenial social clique. One joins a square-dancing group, or a card-playing group, or one enrolls in a course for the study of foreign language, making sure that the other members are persons with whom one will enjoy himself. Especially in the suburbs one might expect couples in their thirties to choose expressive forms of education.

Exerting and Asserting Oneself. Age 40-50

During this decade a person is generally at the peak of his life-cycle, even though he may have more actual power later on. He exerts his maximum energy, and has a choice of ways in which to exert it. A woman is no longer "tied down" to her children. She can be active in clubs, or she can take a job, or she can spend more time with her husband, or she can turn to church or Girl Scout work. The activities of citizenship take more of a person's time in this decade than they ever have before. Homemaking becomes more important in the sense of creating and maintaining a pleasant place in which to live. A person who has leadership potential commences to assert his leadership at this time, or he probably never does so at all.

Investment of energy by the ego in the "outer" world of work and politics and home and family life pays greater returns than it ever has before. However, the situation in which a person finds himself begins to produce difficulties for many persons in this decade, warning of more to come. It is largely the bodily situation which causes difficulties at this time, for the social situation in which a person lives and works is generally favorable at this age.

The body changes of the menopause affect women, with consequent changes in the ego. However, these changes do not necessarily have negative consequences. A woman may become more free to exert and assert herself after the menopause. Her sex life may become more satisfactory, and she may feel more free to assume roles of worker and club-woman, now that the role of mother becomes less important and demanding.

Women as well as men commence to lose physical attractiveness during this decade unless they exert themselves to maintain a youthful appearance. Health problems appear increasingly. Toward the end of this decade, heart attacks begin to take a toll among men, and ulcers also increase in frequency.

Nevertheless, the decade of the 40's is experienced by most people positively, as a period of expansion of their power and influence. In terms of adult education, it is a period of growing interest in civic and cultural study and activity. Women become more active club members, as do men.

From the point of view of the adult educator, the two decades from 40 to 60 pose a problem of motivation for education. The two developmental tasks which provide the highest motivation for instrumental forms of education are past—the tasks of becoming a competent worker and of rearing children. From this time on the tasks of becoming an informed and responsible citizen and of making a comfortable home move into focus, but these tasks seldom have as intense social pressure and individual aspiration behind them as the earlier ones. This is also a period of life when the roles of club or association member and of church member may assume more importance; these also are roles which have less motivation behind them than the roles of worker and parent.

People tend to drop out of adult education activity by the age of 40, and new members are not easy to find.

The principal sources of new participation in adult education are:

> Women who want training for jobs, now that their children are grown up.
>
> People who turn to civic activity and want to study political and economic problems.
>
> People who want to spend more time on activities associated with homemaking, such as gardening, interior decorating, and planning and building a new home.

The growing amount of leisure provides people in this age period with time to do things, but not with new sources of motivation. The expressive forms of adult education might be expected to flourish in such a situation. Theater and play-reading groups, music groups and music appreciation courses, travel and travel-study groups, and a variety of friendship forming and friendship maintaining groups are often attractive to people aged 40 to 60.

At the same time, the people who have formed the habits of self-initiated study will continue in these habits during this period of their lives; if the schools are succeeding in making larger numbers of such people, they will figure more and more prominently in programs of adult education. It would be useful at this time to study a group of self-initiating learners to find out how their educational interests develop during the life cycle. Do they become more interested in economic and political problems at this time, or do they tend to go in for the "cultural" forms of activity?

Maintaining Position and Changing Roles. Age 50-60

The most interesting and the most baffling of the decades of adult life is that of the 50's. By this age the situation of the individual is definitely losing its earlier advantages. Starting with a decline of physical strength and skill and attractiveness in the early 50's, the body becomes less and less favorable for the operation of the ego. People discover limits to what their bodies can do. By the end of the 50's, the libidinal fires begin to die down in men, and this institutes a grave threat to the ego.

Moreover, the social situation begins to lose its earlier favorable character. It is seldom possible for a person to get promotion in his job. His colleagues are beginning to expect him to "slow down." Actually, this decade is pretty much of a plateau period in terms of the power and influence and productivity of a person, but it does not seem that way to the individual. He feels as though he must exert himself in order to avoid losing ground.

The experiences with the body and with the social situation are accompanied by subtle and far-reaching changes in the ego. No longer does the world seem simple and easy to master if one works at it; it now becomes complex, and the ego begins to have doubts about the possibility of mastery.

A study of the responses of men to a TAT test showed this kind of change between the 40's and the 50's. As reviewed by Neugarten,[10] the differences were as follows.

30

"The most frequent stories given by men in the 40 to 49 age group were those in which virility and resistance to coercion were stressed, and in which there was energetic and motoric approach to the environment. Intrusive energies were ascribed to the hero figures; passive and dependent wishes were denied; problems were thrashed out in combative interaction with the environment. Stories given by 50-year-olds were frequently those in which passive and deferent, rather than rebellious or defiant, heroes were projected. The stories of 50-year-olds frequently reflected conflict, in which short-range, sensual, and affiliative rewards were favored over long-range achievement goals; yet in which there was reluctance to retreat from the struggle with outer-world demands."

During this decade the ego turns inward toward the self, and thought begins to replace action as a mode of dealing with the world. Several studies of adults show increased introversion in the late 40's or the early 50's. An example of the ego changes now taking place is the attitude toward the future, which changes radically from the 40's to the 50's. Most people in their 40's think of the future as indefinitely long. They plan to do a large number of things in the future as though there would never be an end, for them. The change which comes with the 50's makes the future seem to be a short period of time, in which there may not be time to do everything one wants to do. Consequently, the 50-year-old commences to give priorities among his projects. He plans the most important ones first, knowing that he may not have time to do everything he would like to do.

Perhaps the most important activity for the future happiness of the individual during this decade is the slow changing of roles that he manages while maintaining his position at the peak of his power and influence in his family, community, and profession. The person who started the decade as the president of his company, the head of his department, the active head of his family, or the president of his community organization, may still be struggling to hold on to these positions, or may have changed to other equally satisfactory and influential roles which are easier to maintain.

A woman who has been an effective mother and head of a growing family of children at 50 is likely to be a grandmother at 60. If she tries to maintain the role she held at 50 she is having trouble; but if she shifts gracefully to the grandmother role she is likely to be happier and more influential.

A man who was at the peak of his working ability at the age of 50 may have passed his prime in specific work skills, but the added wisdom and experience at age 60 may make him a more effective worker, if he learns how to use his wisdom and experience.

The secret of competence during this decade seems to lie in the changing of roles to take advantage of increased experience and to avoid the disadvantages of decreased physical vigor and attractiveness.

Adult education has yet to discover its mission for people in their 50's. In addition to providing for the self-initiating learners, probably it should search for ways of helping people to get perspective on themselves and their careers, and to make the role changes that lead to increased effectiveness and happiness.

Deciding Whether To Disengage and How. Age 60-70

On the whole, people in their 50's maintain their social effectiveness quite well, using the devices described above. They experience an ego-change, but this is not clearly visible to others.

In the 60's, however, there are more visible changes, both in the ego and in social effectiveness. The situation in which the ego operates is now tending to deteriorate for the great majority of people. Body and health become sources of weakness for many people. Most men lose their jobs during this period, some by choice, but most by the working of an arbitrary retirement policy. Most women lose their husbands before the end of this decade. Although this situational change for a woman is not always a misfortune, it practically always forces a reorganization of her life, and a reorganization of her ego.

The crisis during this decade for most people is the crisis of disengagement. This is a process of decreasing interaction between the person and others in society. When a person loses the role of worker or spouse, and becomes less active in the roles of parent, club member, citizen, and church member, he experiences social disengagement. It has been proposed,[2] though not proven, that a process of psychological disengagement takes place as a part of intrinsic or maturational ego development, and gives rise to social disengagement. Psychological disengagement consists of a lessened desire for social approval, increased tendency to select short-run gratifications, such as sweets or entertainment which is easily available and requires no advance planning, and a withdrawal from

32

intensive emotional attachments to people and objects.

The nature of the interaction between social and psychological dis-engagement needs further investigation, but there is no doubt that the 60's is a period when social disengagement occurs with increasing intensity, and the ego becomes involved in conflict over the desirability of the process. A great many people resist the idea of disengagement at first, and continue to resist it as long as they can. A person refuses to retire from employment, and seeks other jobs when he is automatically retired from his main career job. A person holds onto his offices in his church or clubs, in spite of gentle hints that it is time to make way for younger people.

Some people become quite jealous of and hostile to their younger colleagues at work as they reach this period of life. They become critical and bitter. There are some studies of attitudes toward old age and aging that show a great deal of ambivalence and of inconsistency of attitudes by people around the age of 65. Their attitudes were stable for 20 years up to the age of 60, and they develop a new and stable set of attitudes by the age of 70; but the period of the 60's is one of inner conflict for them.

Some people disengage very easily and readily. They have been passive dependent people for whom the effort to be an active and effective participant in the roles of society was unpleasant. Other people fight bitterly against disengagement. Their self-respect depends on their maintaining activity and influence. As a rule, the beginning of the 60's is a period when most people feel and resist the pressures to disengage, coming from their own bodies and from the social environment. But by the end of the 60's it is no longer a question of whether to disengage, but how to do so comfortably, gaining rather than losing by the process. What roles should one give up or reduce, and what satisfactions should one strive to retain or to gain?

The writer and his colleagues[6] have studied the process of disengagement in people between the ages of 50 and 90. They find that social and psychological disengagement take place as people go beyond age 50, and that the process intensifies after the age of 70. That is, there is a slow and gradual process of disengagement between 50 and 70, which often consists of losing certain roles and replacing them with greater activity in other roles. For example, a man becomes more active as a citizen or a club member when he retires from work; or a woman upon becoming a widow becomes more active as a neighbor or club member. Some people do not become disengaged at all until about the age of 70, while others begin the process in their 50's.

After the age of 70, nearly everybody disengages rather rapidly, especially from work activity and from other community activities.

Although the process of disengagement is more or less a relentless one, the evidence is clear that most people who disengage least rapidly are happier than those who disengage rapidly. In general, life satisfaction is higher for people with more activity, or more engagement. However, this is merely a statistical finding. There are some people with very low engagement who are quite happy and satisfied with life, but they are in the minority.

How should adult education be organized for people in their 60's, in the light of what we know about the disengagement process? In attempting to answer this question we are moving into one of the frontier areas of adult education.

One possibility is to focus study groups and counselling on the process of disengagement, for people in their late 50's and early 60's. This is the procedure being used by a number of companies and labor unions in their programs of pre-retirement education. There are now a number of course outlines with readings for people of various levels of sophistication. Several universities are training group leaders and counsellors for this kind of work.

Such courses when they are most successful seem to combine expressive with instrumental features. That is, they work instrumentally to help the individual take stock of himself, his interests, his health, his finances, so as to plan for role changes and for new activities to replace the ones he is giving up; and at the same time they work expressively to give the individual a feeling of companionship with others who are "in the same boat" with him and a feeling of optimism about his future.

Another type of educational activity is a course or set of readings that prepare a person explicitly for the compensatory activities he has chosen to take the place of activities he is giving up—such activities as planning for a round-the-world trip, planning for a winter residence in

34

a warm climate, gardening, and learning new games.

The educational programs discussed up to this point have been age graded—they are for people who are in the late 50's or in their 60's and who have a common interest in meeting the process of disengagement competently. There are other educational activities which are attractive to people at this age as well as to people of other adult age periods. These are: classes and study groups in international relations, domestic economic, and political problems; cultural activities dealing with music, art, dramatics; and the social activities of churches, clubs, and other associations.

Most people in their 60's prefer a mixed age group to an age-graded group. They prefer to see themselves in an adult group with people of all ages rather than to identify themselves with the older age group. These people may accept a short-term study-group on preparation for retirement because of what they expect in the way of assistance with a problem they recognize, but they still prefer to associate with a wider age group. They are learning to disengage slowly and with some resistance from the activities and associations of middle age. Toward the close of the 60's, they begin to accept the idea of disengagement and to use the process constructively for their own satisfaction. At this time they also accept age-graded associations and activities more readily.

Making the Most of Disengagement. Age 70-90

During the final ten or twenty years of life, for that half of the population of a modern society who reach the age of 70 and go beyond that mark, there is a new outlook on life which is more satisfactory to the ego than the two decades which have gone before. Erikson calls this the achievement of "integrity." For Charlotte Buhler it is a sense of "self-fulfillment," when the life-work is completed, and one can live in the present and the past without worrying about the future.

By this time a person has achieved or has accepted a state of disengagement from the active social roles of middle age, and has formed a new and final pattern of engagement in roles that are less demanding of effort to relate to the complexity of social interaction in the modern world. If his body is reasonably healthy, and his social and economic situation reasonably stable and secure, his ego operates freely and with considerable satisfaction. Generally a person at this age needs family or friends for linkage to the social world, and spends a good deal of time and a good deal of his available energy in routines of home and personal life which would have seemed unimportant 20 years earlier.

There is probably a good deal of difference between the sexes in their characteristic ways of managing their lives during this period. Men seem to become more introverted than women, and to rely more on "thinking" to cope with the situations of later life. At least this is the conclusion drawn from personality studies of men and women in their 70's and 80's. Men seem to give up the active and responsible leadership roles more fully than women. Perhaps this is due to the fact that women retain the role of housekeeper as a central role generally as long as they live and also they are more actively engaged in relations with their children and grandchildren.

More study is needed of the differences between men and women in the later years. Why is it that women seem to become "the stronger sex" after the 60's? Are the causes primarily biological, or primarily social?

Educational programs should primarily serve to improve life satisfaction after the age of 70. But in working out such programs we come up against the two opposing theories of successful aging—the "stay young, keep active" theory and the "rocking-chair" theory.

The proponent of the rocking-chair theory would say that a program to enhance life satisfaction should concentrate on making the social situation as comfortable as possible and giving all the health service that is possible. The proponent of the stay young, keep active theory would favor a program of group activities, such as Golden Age clubs, classes in painting, travel in groups, and opportunity for informal social activities.

In our studies of disengagement we have gone far enough to recognize that there are different personality types among older people, and that an activity program will fit certain personality types, while a passive and dependent personality type will prefer the rocking chair. A person's history of dominant concerns and his ways of satisfying them will probably give the best clues to the kind of program he would like to have in his last decade of life.

In any case, this period of life can be a thoroughly satisfactory one for most people, far more satisfying to the individual than is supposed by most younger people.

36

Conclusion

The foregoing analysis of the adult part of the life cycle shows that there are educational needs not now met by adult education. The people with these needs are largely either in the working-class part of society or past 50 years of age.

The challenges to adult education, as seen on the basis of this kind of analysis are:

1. To find ways of extending adult education beyond its instrumental forms into forms which have more expressive or intrinsic values.

2. To find ways of serving more people beyond the age of 50.

3. To find ways of serving more working-class people.

References

1. Bühler, Charlotte, Psychologie im Leben unserer Zeit. Munich: Droemer-Knaur, 1962.

2. Cumming, Elaine and Henry, William E., Growing Old. New York: Basic Books, 1961.

3. Erickson, Erik H., Childhood and Society. Chapter 7, New York: Norton, 1950.

4. Havighurst, Robert J., Human Development and Education. New York: Longmans, Green (David McKay), 1953.

5. Havighurst, Robert J. and Orr, Betty, Adult Needs and Adult Education. Chicago: Center for the Study of Liberal Education for Adults, 1956.

6. Havighurst, Robert J., Neugarten, Bernice L. and Tobin, Sheldon S., "Disengagement and Patterns of Aging." Paper read at the International Congress of Gerontology, Copenhagen, 1963.

7. Kleemeier, Robert, ed., Aging and Leisure, Chapter 11, "The Nature and Values of Meaningful Free-time Activity," by R. J. Havighurst. New York: Oxford University Press, 1961.

8. Lipset, S. M., Political Man: The Social Bases of Politics. New York: Doubleday, 1960.

9. Miller, S. M. and Riessman, Frank, "The Working-Class Sub-Culture: A New View." Social Problems. Summer, 1961.

10. Neugarten, Bernice L., "Personality Changes during the Adult Years" in Psychological Backgrounds of Adult Education. Chicago: Center for the Study of Liberal Education for Adults, 1963.

11. Thorndike, E. L., Human Nature and the Social Order. New York: Macmillan, 1940.

CHANGING VALUE ORIENTATIONS IN ADULT LIFE

Eugene A. Friedmann
Brown University

The Study of Values

A value according to one widely cited definition "is a conception explicit or implicit, of the desirable which influences the selection from available modes, means and ends of action" (Kluckhohn, 1951). It differs from a purely personal statement of preference or desire in that it reflects what the individual or his group "believe they ought or should desire," and thus it is a part of the body of culturally transmitted norms which regulate human behavior. From the point of view of the individual, values enable him to: 1) select among the various socially approved goals for action and the means of achieving them; and 2) assign priorities among and integrate the various courses of action which are available.

As Kingsley Davis notes, society offers for each person "a multiplicity of goals but only scarce means (time and energy)" for attaining them (1949, p. 243). Personal unity then requires an organization of ends by the individual and a selection of appropriate means. "The person's value system is therefore a network of sovereign but mutually dependent goals. He must know how to give each goal its due, which means he must have . . . a scale of values . . . " (Davis, pp. 244-45). It is this scale that serves as the integrating feature for the individual in the organization of his life pattern serving to allocate his efforts among the available range of means and ends in a manner which renders compatible desires and preferences of his own which may be in conflict, each with the other or with the demands of society.

The study of values may range from considerations of the broadest statements of cultural ideals to the minutest details of individual preference or desires. Further, they may be viewed from the perspective of the individual, of the groups he participates in, or of the entire society itself. Our concern is limited in two ways. First we will be dealing with value patterns as they influence behavior in the adult portion of the life span of the individual in our society. In particular we will consider the values which are clustered around the major institutionalized roles of the adult years—work, family, community, etc. And, second, we will be further limiting our considerations to changes in values and value scales or priorities as they may typically occur with passage through the several stages of adult life.

The concept of value orientations as developed by Florence Kluckhohn has a particular relevance to the investigation of changes which occur through time. As she views it, these are the elements "which give order and direction to the ever-flowing stream of human acts and thoughts as they relate to the solution of 'common human problems'" (1961, p. 4). She further postulates that: 1) there is a common number of human problems which must find solution; 2) the number of possible solutions is limited; 3) societies' (and individuals') value orientations allow the selection of more than one permissible solution; and 4) priorities are assigned to value orientations which arrange them into dominant and variant (alternate) patterns.

Of the five value orientation areas which relate to the solution of common human problems we are selecting three which have particular relevance to the changes in life situation which typically occur through the adult life span and about which existing knowledge permits some inference. The value orientation areas and the variant types of orientations within each area are:

1) Time orientation
   a. Past
   b. Present
   c. Future

2) Activity
   a. Instrumental—concerns activities engaged in not for their own sake but as a means of achieving other goals.[1]
   b. Expressive—concerns activities engaged in for the immediate and direct gratification derived.[1]

3) Relational
   a. Lineal—relationships in a hierarchical patterning of authority determine primacy of goals.

---

1. Here we have departed from Kluckhohn's categories of "being, becoming and doing" and substituted categories suggested by Parsons (1951, p. 209) which are relevant to this area. Some precedent for this usage can be found in the study by Rosen (1956).

40

b.　Collateral—relationships with peer group determine
　　　　　primacy of goals.
　　　c.　Individualistic—individual goals have primacy over-
　　　　　specific collateral or lineal groups.

Our concern with the patterns of value orientations in adult life will
be directed toward:

1.　The determination of typical patterns as reflected in the per-
　　formance of major adult roles in our society.

2.　Cyclical shifts in patterning which occur during the course of
　　performance in specific roles.

3.　The consequences of role loss.

4.　Their influence in the selection of new goals and role activities.

5.　Their relationship to the socialization processes in adulthood.

Value Orientations and Life Cycle Analysis

The life cycle as a unit of social time has been employed extensively
by the anthropologist, dating back to Margaret Mead's early accounts of
the process of growing up in Samoa (1928). As Honigman notes, practically an entire culture can be described from the point of view of the individual as he moves from birth to death (1959, p. 559). It provided for
the anthropologist a way of viewing the phenomena of culture transmission through time as a process of socialization of the young as well as a
framework for the interpretation of the impact of differing modes of child
rearing and socialization upon the behavior and personality of the adult.
The life cycle was marked off into age stages, each defined by the culture
as to its functions, roles, relation to other age stages, duration and points
of entry, and termination.

For the simplest societies, where the family and kin group embrace
almost the entire range of social activity, specialization by age stage and
by sex form the basis of the division of labor, and groupings arranged by
age stage and by sex form the basis of the pattern of social relationships.
In a society of this sort parents and peers provide the individual adequate-
ly for the majority of his future roles. The cycle is defined in terms of
the successive age roles the individual plays in the context of the kin
group and in relationship to community. Each stage has a recognizable
and often ceremonially marked point of entry and exit. Each age stage is

41

assigned tasks and duties which in turn are closely integrated with the activities of the other age stages.

Almost all societies make a distinction between infancy, childhood, adolescence, adulthood, and old age as divisions of the life cycle. Although anthropological research has employed the life cycle concept in a great number of investigations of preliterate and peasant communities, the concept of adulthood is a unitary one in a simple society, consisting of a relatively small number of roles which begin and terminate at roughly the same points. Contemporary society with its high degree of specialization and differentiation of institutional structures is characterized by a multiplicity of adult roles, many of which do not span the entire period of adulthood. Developmental studies in Western societies were focused originally on the infancy-childhood-adolescence portions of the life cycle, then expanded their purview to include old age and just recently have begun to concern themselves with the adult years as viewed in developmental sequence. Therefore, the body of data we have to draw upon for this analysis is inadequate in many respects, and a good many inferences will have to be drawn from studies designed for purposes other than the ones which concern us at this time and which only incidentally shed light upon development in the adult years.

The roles which a person is called upon to play in adult life change as the social positions to which they are related change. In a rigidly structured society the unfolding of adult life can be depicted in terms of a clearly defined sequence of positions which the individual passes. Particularly in a society where positions are ascribed, passage from position to position is guaranteed practically as a reward for survival. In a less rigidly structured society where the individual has greater freedom in selecting and changing his mind about the positions which he wants to achieve (and simultaneously a greater freedom to fail) there will be less certainty in the course which developmental patterns follow. Nevertheless, there will be typical sequences of position as the social system itself acts to set limits upon the orientation of his life pattern. These typical sequences Hughes has termed careers (1937). They are usually thought of in terms of work careers, but can be found in almost any institutionalized sphere of activity. Thus, Hughes notes:

> The woman may have a career in holding together a family or in raising it to a new position. Some people of quite modest occupa-

42

tional achievements have careers in patriotic, religious and civic organizations. They may budget their efforts toward some cherished office of this kind rather than toward advancement in their occupation. It is possible to have a career in an avocation as well as in a vocation.

Role changes marked by entrance into or separation from a major career of course requires major readjustments of life patterns; redefinitions of goals and means of achieving them which bring the pattern of value orientations into play as a selection device; and perhaps a reorganization of the pattern of value priorities themselves as dominant values are replaced by variant ones.

But beginnings and endings are not the only points of role changes in career lines. Careers have achievement sequences which alter the nature of the individual's role, his evaluations of self and his participation in a range of activities which the change in the career position may make it necessary or satisfying for him to engage in. Conversely, the quest for achievement may be of shorter duration than the career line itself. Thus, in the middle years of a work career a man may decide that he has gone as far as he wants, and begin to restructure his goals.

Career Lines and Adult Socialization Processes: A Scheme of Analysis

All societies have provisions for socializing their members in the skills and behaviors expected of them in their roles as adults. In small-scale, simple, homogeneous societies the educational functions are performed by parents, parental relatives, and peers. As societies increase in size and complexity in their divisions of labor the body of knowledge to be transmitted is beyond the capacity of the family to convey. Prior to recent times the school as a formal educational organization influenced the socialization of only a small percentage of the population, limited essentially to the elites of the society.

The extent of specialization in modern societies is based upon an accumulation of knowledge which is not only beyond the capacity of the family to transmit but also beyond that of any organization which is not primarily organized to serve an educational function. It is only in modern society that schooling has become universal. The separating out of the educational function and the creation of a specialized educational organization has had the effect of (1) separating the process of role preparation from the settings of role performance, and (2) sharply restricted

43

the range of roles which this formalized agency of socialization was expected to equip the individual for. Thus, participation in formal educational programs became a preparation for future performance (in contrast to learning a task while doing it) in limited areas of adult participation.

In particular, the American school with its stress upon middle class models of success became a vehicle for equipping the individual to attain future goals through a long career sequence of vocational achievement. In terms of our value orientation scheme of analysis we can describe its time orientation as "future" and its activity orientation as "instrumental." And, further, since in our society it stressed goal achievement through individual effort or through cooperation with a work group its position on the relational scale can be described as "individualistic-collateral."

In the process of adult socialization the school as a formal educational organization has a greatly reduced significance when compared to the pre-adult phase of the life cycle. Adult socialization occurs mainly through the processes of situational learning while engaged in role performance ("on-the-job" learning); or in the preparation for future roles through the influence of other institutional systems and the mass media. Since participation in adult education programs is voluntary, we would expect it to vary according to the degree of compatibility which exists between the value orientations of the program and those of the individual. However, value orientations in adult life are not constant for the individual but rather represent a shifting pattern changing with the nature of his career commitments in the various stages of the life span. It is necessary then for the adult educator to consider the character of typical adult careers in our society and their combinations in the several stages of adult life.

In our society the major adult careers are related to the institutionalized commitments of work and the family. These for most are the goal defining and organizing foci of adult life. We propose to examine these in some detail, and then consider briefly participation in voluntary organizations and selected other activities which may represent careers for some, or relate to the development of major careers.

44

Work Careers

Significance of the Job. Today's youth entering the labor force at age 20, working a 40-hour week and remaining continuously employed until retirement at age 65 will have spent approximately 83,000 hours or about 30 per cent of his adult waking life engaged in job activity. The job, of course, is a major consumer of time in adult life and the means by which economic goods and prestige are obtained in our society. It is the facilitating device for attaining a wide range of life goals outside of the area of work. But by the same token, since job performance is critical to achievement in so many areas, much of the worker's activity off the job as well as his emotional commitments and value orientation are directed toward job accomplishment. Thus "the job in our society exerts an influence which pervades the whole of the human life span. . . . [it] can be regarded as an axis along which the worker's pattern of life is organized. It serves to maintain him in his group, to regulate his life-activity, to fix his position in society, and to determine the pattern of his social participation and the nature of his life experiences, and is a source of many of his satisfactions and affective experiences" (Friedmann and Havighurst, 1954, p. 3). We might expect to find, then, that shifts in roles which occur in the various stages of the work career would result in a realignment of patterns of value orientation, goal selection, and participation in a range of life activities.

Stages in the Work Career. Career lines may vary according to their stability and the extent to which progress through an ascending sequence of job statuses continues through the span of working life. Chart I represents an extreme degree of stability and structuring of progressive statuses throughout a career line, as represented by an army officer's career plan. This career line is atypical in several ways. First, as we have already noted, it is more rigidly structured than most; second, achievement is on an upward plane continuously to the end of the career (the plateau which is reached in the middle or later stages of most careers is eliminated by the service policy of "promote or retire").

Yet, although atypical, it can be regarded as an idealized formulation of the developing stages of a career. It contains almost all of the elements which are found in the first two of the following four stages of analysis of career lines in our society:

CHART I

IDEALIZED CAREER LINE OF ARMY OFFICERS

Stage	Time Span from Entry	Expectations of Position
I. Basic Military Development	0-8 yrs.	a. Grounding in matters pertaining to officer's branch b. Establishing primary proficiency in basic tactical and technical performances
II. Intermediate Professional Development and Re-evaluation	9-15 yrs.	a. Developing proficiency in tactical and technical skills b. Assignments requiring complex face-to-face contact (major staff assignments, schools, command of large organizational elements)
III. Advanced Contribution and Development (also referred to as "period of career realization and advanced professional standing")	16-23 yrs.	a. Tactical, technical proficiencies emphasized in earlier periods now "subordinated to ability to view the Dept. of the Army as a whole" b. Increase in branch immaterial assignments c. Command of small segments
IV. Major Professional Contribution Period	24-30 yrs.	Application of talents to "worldwide problems of strategy" and to policy innovation

Source: Career Planning for Officers, Department of the Army, 1963.

Stage 1. Entry—this typically consists of a period of trial in which the individual (or the employer) determines whether he will commit himself to the career or reject it.

Stage 2. Career development—the period of dedication to learning the techniques for advancement through the mastering of technical skills and/or the skills of manipulating persons in the work situation.

Stage 3. Plateau—begins at the point at which the individual reaches the decision that he has gone about as far up the achievement ladder in his occupational setting as he will reach; resolved by reorienting his pattern of expectations or else by seeking new employment.

Stage 4. Pre-retirement—probably not a clearly defined stage for many workers at this time; but as retirement becomes in-

creasingly institutionalized as an expectation for most it
will have a growing significance as a period of reorientation toward a post-work phase of the life cycle.

Shifts in Value Orientation through the Work Career:[2] Stages I and II.

Time orientation. Since these are both viewed as stages in an upward
climb, the time orientation would be "future." This orientation contains
the convictions that 1) the future will be better than the present; 2) change
in attitudes, skills, and ways of doing things is desirable as a way of improving life in the future; and 3) life can be planned.

Activity orientation. The achievement orientation dominant in these
stages of the career line would fit our "instrumental" category previously
defined.

Relational orientation. If we assume that the individual has had some
preparatory training upon entering his career, possesses some confidence
in the skills he has or his ability to learn skills, and subscribes to the
dominant cultural value that a person can succeed in a career of his own
choosing on the basis of individual merit, we would be justified in rating
the activity orientation in stage I as "individual." The Army career line
presented in Chart I lists the development of individual competence as a
prerequisite for advancement as an expectation for its first stage. But its
frankness in listing the development of competence in "face-to-face" contacts as an expectation of the second stage of the career is, at least in its
implications, a statement "rarely found in official policy statement of organizations" (Dalton, 1959). The shift from "individual" to "collateral" relational orientations in the transition into our second stage of the career
for engineers recruited for managerial training in industry is described
by Dalton:

> Entering industry for the first time, the logical but unsophisticated
> young staff officer is usually shocked to find himself caught in the
> cross fire of staff-line skirmishes that must never come to open
> battle. He expected to engage in specific and clear-cut relations with
> everybody. He assumed his training would lead him to a precise,
> methodical round of duties. Now he finds that his freedom to apply
> himself is checked by shifting arrangements . . . when he . . . [adapts
> to this situation] . . . he is likely to be more concerned with social
> relations to aid his advancement than with creative effort for the firm
> (Dalton, 1959, p. 95).

---

2. The relationships between value orientation, stage of career line,
and socialization process is depicted in Chart II.

CHART II

RELATION BETWEEN STAGES IN THE WORK CAREER, VALUE ORIENTATION
AND SOCIALIZATION PROCESS, FOR MALES

Stage	Approximate Age Range	Work Value Orientation				Socialization Process	
		Time	Relational	Activity	Form	Form	Agent
1. Entry into Career	20-28	Future-Present	Individual-Collateral	Instrumental	Adaptive	Work group
2. Career Development	25-50	Future	Collateral-Lineal	Instrumental	Anticipatory-Adaptive	Work group, formal education
3. Plateau	35-60	Present	Collateral-Individual	Expressive-Instrumental	Adaptive	Work group
4. Pre-Retirement	55-68	Present	Individual-Collateral	Expressive-Instrumental	Adaptive-Anticipatory	Work group, formal education, mass media

48

If we follow the logic of Reisman's "other-directed" man or Whyte's "organization man" we might assume that this is the dominant relational mode in both of the career line stages. That this phenomenon is not confined to the large scale, bureaucratized "organization man" type of occupational setting is indicated by Hall in his study of the stages of a medical career. The problem faced by the physician in what would be our second stage of the career line he describes as X's being accepted into the "inner fraternity of medical practice" (Hall, 1947). The physician should be technically competent; however, admission is not based upon technical competence but upon his ability to demonstrate that he shares the collective goals and values of the "inner fraternity." And, finally, at the level of the manual occupations Chinoy has described a comparable shift from "individualistic" to "collateral" orientations in the career lines of automobile workers (Chinoy, 1955).

Stage III: Arrival at the "plateau" stage, characterized by the renunciation of work career achievement aspirations, occurs at varying ages according to the structuring of opportunities within a given work career, the strength of his achievement commitment and the degree of success he has had in mastering the techniques of advancement within a given career line. Unlike the idealized diagram of the army career, the plateau is reached in most occupational career lines sometime before retirement and frequently in the middle years of life. Chinoy's study of factory workers in the automobile industry revealed that they had a limited range of aspirations and that those who remained in the limited opportunity structure of assembly line work reached a plateau in their late 30's (Chinoy, 1955). Miller and Form (1951) in a study of a series of occupations put the plateau at the late 20's for manual workers, the early 30's for clerical workers, and the late 50's for proprietors, officials, managers, and professionals.

We could speculate that the shift in time orientation at the plateau would be from "future" to "present." Chart II describes the activity orientation as shifting from "instrumental" to "expressive-instrumental." The "instrumental" component has a somewhat different meaning in each case, however. In the ascending stage of the career, current job activity is instrumental in attaining achievement objectives on the job career line as well as instrumental in obtaining the source of income for the entire range of life activities. At the plateau stage it is the achievement instru-

49

mentality component that drops out. The introduction of the "expressive" element would require some degree of stress upon the intrinsic values of work. That work had meaning for the individual beyond its instrumental significance of income has been shown by meaning of work studies of persons in the plateau stage. Some observers have also suggested that at this stage the individual redirects his interests toward participation and achievement in the non-work areas of his life pattern. The collateral relational orientations built up in earlier phases persist along with the building of an "individualistic" orientation.

Stage IV: The pre-retirement stage can only be discussed in a most tentative fashion, since we do not know the extent to which workers presently conceive of this as a stage. To the extent that it is so regarded, its time orientation might be "present"; activity orientation could be "expressive-instrumental"; and the relational orientation might begin to stress "individual" over "collateral."

Variant Work Careers. Our idealized model of a career was that of a stairway of job statuses within a single occupation and within a single organization. Yet, such neat patterns of progression are probably common only in the career lines of a relatively small number of persons, usually in the lower to middle managerial echelons of large, bureaucratically structured organizations and possibly in the career lines of many professional workers.

What of the man who improves his job status by changing organizations? Or by moving into another occupation? And what of the man who switches jobs or occupations that represent no "improvement" in status when tabulated in the usual labor force categories used for this purpose? That occupational shifts are common was shown in results of the Lipset-Bendix survey of labor force mobility for males in Oakland, California, (Bendix, Lipset, 1959) and summarized here in Table 1. In this sample no occupational group other than professional workers had spent as much as 50 per cent of the work careers in a single occupational grouping. As to the frequency of job shifts, the same survey used 2-5 job shifts per decade at its medium mobility category. While upward mobility generally exceeds downward mobility, it is significant to note that 60 per cent of the job shifts were within the same occupational grouping. Unrepresented in any statistical data are the countless number of positional shifts which occur in a given job—e.g., from secretary to the second vice-president,

TABLE 1

PERCENTAGE OF RESPONDENTS WHO SPENT DESIGNATED
PROPORTIONS OF THEIR WORK CAREERS IN THEIR
PRESENT OCCUPATIONAL GROUP
(Excludes female respondents and males 30 and younger)

Occupational Group of Present Job	Proportion of Work Career in Present Occupational Group			Number of Respondents
	80-100%	50-79%	Under 50%	
Professional	70	9	22	23
Semiprofessional	47	32	21	19
Own business	11	31	57	105
Upper white collar	14	21	65	72
Lower white collar	18	33	49	67
Sales	26	24	50	42
Skilled	22	35	43	169
Semiskilled	22	29	49	98
Unskilled	18	21	61	44
Manual	65[a]	21	14	314[b]
Nonmanual	58[a]	23	19	343[b]
All groups	22	29	50	657

[a]The proportion of all manual or all nonmanual workers who have
spent 80-100 per cent of their time in these categories is, of course,
higher than the corresponding proportion for the separate occupational
groups. Shifting between jobs may be frequent without entailing a cross-
over from the manual to the nonmanual occupations, or vice versa.

[b]These figures include 15 business executives and 3 manual (odd-
job) workers not shown separately.

Source: S. M. Lipset and R. Bendix, Social Mobility in Industrial
Society, Heinemann Books on Sociology, 1959, p. 161.

to secretary to the first vice-president.

The definition of work career most suitable for our purposes must
take into account the chronology of occupational, job, and the more subtle
shifts in position which occur within a particular job setting: the sequence
of jobs and job positions which the individual occupies during the span of
his labor force participation.

Socialization Processes in the Stages of the Work Career.

The analysis of the relationship between formal education programs
and their participants must be considered in the context of the total range
of socializing influences which are operative in adult life. Socialization,

the orientation of the person to his social world, is a continuous process operating through the entire life span. Our considerations will be limited to the influence of three of the various instruments which are operative: 1) the peer group; 2) the mass media; and 3) formal education.

The peer group is regarded as the group of social equals with whom the individual participates.

The mass media includes all forms of cultural dissemination which are intended to influence individuals as members of an audience (i.e., persons having no structured interaction with each other or with the communicator). This usage is broader than some, and is intended to include not only television, radio, and newspapers but also books, theater, and the arts (insofar as it is the product of the artist that is being displayed), public lectures and exhibits, etc.

Formal education is used to describe any structured activity which has continuity, a clientele, and regards education as its major function. Thus, we would include not only the programs of the school, but also specialized educational programs of churches, industry, labor unions, and other voluntary associations. Finally, adaptive socialization refers to the process of orienting the individual to his current role; anticipatory socialization refers to preparations made by the individual for roles he may occupy in the future. Anticipatory socialization would characterize the stages of the work cycle up to the plateau; adaptive socialization would occur at all stages.

The mass media and peer group are significant agencies of socialization at all stages of the work career. Formal educational programs lose their significance after the reaching of the plateau. This is not surprising as their function is to equip the individual with skills for future in the work career. But what is puzzling is the fact that male participation in school sponsored education programs seems to drop off sharply by about age 40. Since the career development stage of the work cycle continues well beyond this age in the professional, official, proprietor and manager occupational categories, and may continue past this age at other occupational levels as well, it would seem that vocational education would still be relevant. At this point, then, we can try to put to test the analytical model we have been constructing and see what kind of hypotheses can be derived to account for this phenomenon.

Starting with the historical observation that the contemporary school is unique in that it separates vocational preparation from task perform-ance, we could expect that the values it transmits are the dominant, uni-versal cultural themes rather than those which are related to life situa-tions. In this case the dominant themes are equality of opportunity, free-dom of choice in selection of goals, the possibility of long upward career gradients, and success through individual merit and performance in tech-nical skills. Or in our terminology: future, instrumental, and individual-istic value orientations. If this is the value orientation of adult vocational education as well, then on the basis of our initial propositions about the relationship between compatibility in institutional and individual value ori-entations to participation, and proceeding from our analysis of changing value orientations in the adult work career, we can offer the following re-lational statements for test:

Hypothesis 1: Participation in school sponsored adult vocational edu-cation programs will vary inversely with the length of time that the indi-vidual has been committed to a given career line. We would expect that participation would be greatest for persons who: 1) are first establishing a work career commitment, or 2) who have experienced a major break in their career line and are making a new career commitment. The first test receives some support from available data on age changes in male participation. There is no available data, unfortunately, which relates to the second test, but it could be readily obtained.

Hypothesis 2: During the second (career-development stage) of the career, participation in vocational education will vary according to the degree of sanction received from the participant's work peer group.

This, I believe, is a most important hypothesis for testing; both for the bearing it may have upon adult education enrollment and, more impor-tant, for possible significance it may have for the role of adult education in keeping middle career men abreast of the rapid changes in our tech-nology. During this stage the time and activity orientations are the same as in the first stage which would make "anticipatory socialization" (voca-tional training) appropriate, but the relational setting in which it becomes acceptable to the individual has been altered. Thus, at the outset of the work career where the individualistic orientation is dominant the worker will participate in programs without reference to the opinions of his work group. But as he becomes enmeshed in the network of collateral relation-

53

ships, the approval of the work group becomes more important.

Will he be regarded as pushy or impatient if he participates on his own, or will his desire for training be regarded as evidence of a lack of competence? The answer then would be to obtain not just the formal approval of the work group but some basic degree of acceptance by the inner-fraternity of peers referred to by Hall. At this point the approval or possible co-sponsorship of professional and occupational societies would be helpful. This procedure has been followed with some success in the training of doctors, lawyers, and bankers already established in their career lines. Would the same degree of success have been achieved without such colleagueal sanction? And, even more important, how can the skilled workers and technicians whose skills are being rapidly outdated by the current technological revolution be reached? Our analysis indicates that 30 or 35 would be a better age than 50 to begin such retraining; but again the problem may be that of altering a pattern of peer group concensus rather than motivating the worker as an isolated member of a mass society.

Family Careers of the Married Woman

Many a mother in Crestwood Heights stated somewhat ruefully that motherhood had "cut short" her career. She was unlikely to think of motherhood itself as a career, even though she felt that she was doing a good job as wife and mother. If questioned directly, she would aver that motherhood was a career, but she would omit mention of housekeeping, unless closely questioned as to her attitude towards it. Then, although she might not dismiss housekeeping as plain drudgery and lament the lack of domestic help, she would nevertheless qualify her acceptance of housekeeping by linking it to the other ends: child-rearing, making her husband happy, or her interest in entertaining.

(Seeley, Sims and Loosely, Crestwood Heights, 1956)

Marriage and child rearing may represent an interrupted work career if we consider that our educational system prepares women for work, that a majority of them are employed at some time before their marriage, and that they are entering the labor force in increasing numbers when their children are in later stages of childhood. But still the percentage employed is not higher than 39 per cent for any stage of the marriage career (Table 2) and the majority of women who work seem to be doing so to meet a short term financial need rather than a long term commitment to a work career (Sobol in Nye and Hoffman, 1963).

The family career line of the woman is closely intertwined with

54

TABLE 2

PER CENT OF WOMEN IN THE LABOR FORCE BY STAGE IN FAMILY CYCLE, 1940-1960

	1940	1944	1948	1952	1955	1958	1960
Single	48.1	58.6	51.1	50.0	46.6	45.4	44.1
Married, living with husband	14.7	21.7	22.0	25.3	27.7	30.2	30.5
No children under 18			28.4	30.9	32.7	38.8	34.7
Children 6-17 only			26.0	31.1	34.7	37.6	39.0
Children 0-5	8.6[1]	... [2]	10.7	13.9	16.0	18.2	18.6
Widowed, divorced, living apart	35.4	42.0	38.3	38.8	38.5	40.8	40.0
All women	25.7	35.0	31.0	32.7	33.4	35.0	34.8

Sources: Current Population Reports, Labor Force (4) and Special Labor Force Report No. 13 (14).

[1]Estimated. Source: Women as Workers (15).

[2]No information available.

From: F. Ivan Nye and Lois Hoffman, Rand McNally & Co., 1963, The Employed Mother in America.

those of her husband and children and has less of the self directing momentum that characterizes the employment career of the male. It is further characterized by sharp breaks in family composition at several points, each requiring a major role reorientation on her part. For our purposes the description of a modal and hypothetical family with two children will be useful. (See Chart II and Tables 2 and 3.)

Stage 1. Married Pair Age of entry: 20 years Duration: 2 years

This is a brief period of establishing the marriage, forming the household, and preparing for the arrival of children. The time orientation may stress either "present" or "future" depending upon point at which the commitment to the family as a career is made. The relational orientation is collateral with a rapid dropping out of lineal elements as the break with the parental generation is made, as the lateral bond between husband and wife is reinforced, and as lateral friendship associations are expanding. The activity orientation would be expressive both in the sense that Zelditch has used it, i.e., the stabilizing source of emotional response and gratification (Zelditch in Parson and Bales, 1955), and in the

TABLE 3

MEDIAN AGE OF HUSBAND AND WIFE AT SELECTED STAGES
OF THE LIFE CYCLE OF THE FAMILY: 1890 AND 1950

Stage of the Life Cycle of the Family	Median Age of Husband		Median Age of Wife	
	1950	1890	1950	1890
A. First marriage	22.8	26.1	20.1	22.0
B. Birth of last child	28.8	36.0	26.1	31.9
C. Marriage of last child	50.3	59.4	47.6	55.3
D. Death of one spouse[1]	64.1	57.4	61.4	53.3
E. Death of other spouse[2]	71.6	66.4	77.2	67.7

[1]Husband and wife survive jointly from marriage to specified age.

[2]Husband (wife) survives separately from marriage to specified age.

Source: Paul C. Glick "The Life Cycle of the Family," Marriage and Family Living, Vol. XVII, No. 1, February 1955, p. 4.

sense of seeking gratification of immediate desires, as we have defined it.

Stage 2. Child Rearing Age of entry: 22 years Duration: 25 years

This is a period with many substages representing significant alterations in roles and probably shouldn't be subsumed under one stage. This would also be the period of job career commitment and development for the husband, and the wife would in varying degrees become involved in it. This is also the period of establishing relationships with neighbors and friends in the neighborhood of settlement, of activity in child oriented organizations, and of entry into and the development of participation career lines in an assortment of community organizations. In the later years of this stage the highest rates of labor force participation by women are reached (Table 3).

Value orientations for the women would reach their strongest future time orientation in this period as they assume their major child-rearing role; similarly the activity orientation would stress instrumental values; the relational variable would be collateral-lineal as she maintains and reinforces her friendship and peer group participation ties and also assumes lineal authoritarian responsibilities in the rearing of the child.

Socialization in the many roles she plays would be strongly influenced by the peer group (particularly if she lives in a neighborhood where families are of the same stage of family development); also the influence of the mass media is strong, particularly in view of the stress upon reaching her as the key buyer in the economy which is evidenced in the content of many magazines and much television programing. Formal education participation is adaptive in terms of problems of child rearing and household management.

Stage 3. <u>Post-child rearing couple</u> Age of entry: 47 years
Duration: 14 years

This is an entirely new phase in the life cycle for woman in the western world. Glick's data (Table 2) indicate that in 1890 the death of one spouse would have occurred on the average of 2 years <u>before</u> this stage would be reached. In this idealized modal couple it could represent a period of release. Child responsibilities and expenses have largely ended; the tensions associated with the career development stage of the husband's work career have been resolved. Present, expressive, and collateral value orientations would be stressed. Socialization would be adaptive and anticipatory.

Stage 4. <u>Widowhood</u> Age of entry: 64 years Duration: 14 years

This stage requires, of course, an adjustment to loss of spouse, the possibility of living alone, a decreasing energy level, a decreasing circle of friends and area of life activity, and a varying rate of withdrawal from previous patterns of participation. The rate and extent of a decline is highly variable, however, and some maintain a fairly full round of life activities while others may withdraw at a rapid rate. The time orientation would be present or perhaps past, the activity orientation would be expressive, and the relational orientation would be shifting from collateral to individualism. The socialization process would be adaptive. Activities would be selected in terms of the gratification of present needs. If the time orientation is past, however, activity selection might be upon the basis of identification with a cherished tradition or heritage. Adult education in this first instance would be able to offer participation in hobbies and crafts, the arts or any appropriate content that would give a direct satisfaction to the participant. In the second instance of past orientation, local history might be of interest to a long time resident of an area (with perhaps a chance to carry on an individual or small group project) or when appropriate, such things as music, poetry, or literature.

The second and third stages above are periods of relatively high participation in formal educational activity. The significance of the expressive-collateral orientation should be tested further and suggests the following hypothesis:

Hypothesis 3: <u>Individuals characterized by an expressive activity value orientation and a collateral relational value orientation will select education programs in terms of intrinsic satisfactions derived and a satisfying interaction with the group.</u>

This differs in significance from the collateral-instrumental orientation referred to in Hypothesis 2. In that case participation would be determined by reference to a group external to the program. In the present combination participation would be determined by the extent of the individual's integration into the group. Thus, we are suggesting that participation in this family career stage may be selected as much in terms of the sociability and congeniality of the group, as by the content of the program.

Education and the Adult Life Span

Shifting Goals and Participation in Adult Education

The school in our society is charged with preparing the young for their adult roles. Its initial concern is for the very young whose life paths appear as a single broad highway and whose aspirations relate to the attainment of goals in a relatively distant future. It seeks to transmit a sufficient portion of the cultural heritage to allow the individual to function effectively as a member of society and, more specifically, to prepare him for future participation in the major work, family, and citizenship spheres of adult life. As the youth approaches adulthood, goals become increasingly differentiated and specific in character. The more advanced phases of his education are oriented toward the attainment of selected goal objectives; the selection usually in terms of the achievement of vocational goals as the key determinant of success in our society or, to a much lesser extent, the attainment of family goals.

We have selected for our analysis the basic careers of work and family which have traditionally defined the role of the adult in our society. To the extent that adult education is related to training in work and family

58

role competencies, we have seen that it is directed to career lines which do not cover the span of adult life. Thus, the male, retiring today at age 65 would have a life expectancy of about 13 years or approximately 23 per cent of his adult life to be spent in the post retirement phase of the life cycle. And if we further assume that for most men the plateau in the work career is reached between the ages of 35 and 55 we now have a span of from 20 to 40 years, or 36 per cent to 72 per cent of the adult life during which education for job advancement is no longer relevant. Similarly, as our family cycle data indicated (Table 2), the woman now completing her major adult task of child rearing in her late 40's would still have 30 years or 39 per cent of her adult life to be spent in the post child rearing phase of the life cycle; a period during which conventional family life education would, of course, have no relevance.

The decreasing age of termination of the work and child rearing phases of the life cycle during the century as well as of the decline in relevance of vocational education for the male in the middle years of his work life is of the utmost significance for adult education. First, it represents the bulk of adults in middle age as well as old age for whom the traditional "vocational-education-for-men" and "family-education-for-women" program formats are no longer relevant. Secondly, demographic changes occurring in this century have resulted in a steadily increasing proportion of middle aged and older adults in the composition of the adult population itself. Thus, Table 4 describing the changing age composition within the adult population indicates that the 45-64 year old group—women have completed the child-rearing phase of the family cycle, and men have completed the career development phase of the work cycle—has increased since 1900 from 25 per cent to 33 per cent of the adult population. Similarly, the 65 year and over age group has increased from 7 per cent to 15 per cent of the adult population in the same period. Combining these figures we find the proportion of the adult population 45 years and over has increased from 32 per cent to 48 per cent of the adult population; and projections indicate that by 1970 approximately half of the potential market for adult education will be with adults, 45 years and over. Lastly, the fact that the adult educator is failing to reach this group is documented by national surveys of adult participation such as those conducted by the U.S. Bureau of the Census (Holden, 1958) or N.O.R.C. (Johnstone, infra), which indicate a progressive decline in adult participation after age 40.

TABLE 4

DISTRIBUTION OF ADULT (20 YEARS OF AGE AND OVER) U.S. POPULATION BY AGE, 1900-1960
(%)

Age	1900	1910	1920	1930	1940	1950	1960
Male							
20-44	67.71	67.07	63.93	61.92	58.81	56.82	52.92
45-64	25.14	25.78	28.35	29.34	30.98	31.33	33.31
65+	7.15	7.15	7.72	8.74	10.21	11.85	13.77
	100.00	100.00	100.00	100.00	100.00	100.00	100.00
Female							
20-44	68.29	67.69	65.86	63.37	59.90	57.02	51.67
45-64	24.23	24.60	26.07	27.69	29.42	30.21	32.69
65+	7.48	7.71	8.07	8.94	10.68	12.77	15.64
	100.00	100.00	100.00	100.00	100.00	100.00	100.00
Total							
20-44	67.99	67.37	64.87	62.64	59.35	56.92	52.27
45-64	24.70	25.21	27.24	28.52	30.20	30.76	32.99
65+	7.31	7.42	7.89	8.84	10.45	12.32	14.74
	100.00	100.00	100.00	100.00	100.00	100.00	100.00

The reasons why adult participation in educational programing drops rapidly past age 40 or 45 are not altogether clear. Our earlier suggested test of compatibility or "goodness of fit" between the goals and value orientations of contemporary adult education structures and those of its audience can be applied here with some suggestive results.

Our life cycle analysis indicated, that with the exception of the woman seeking to reenter the labor force when her children have reached adulthood, vocational education loses its relevance for the adult when he reaches his 40's. Johnstone's data on adult participation supports the contention that nonvocational motives for participation characterize the older rather than the younger adult. Yet surveys of university extension education (e.g., Morton, 1953) indicate that perhaps three-quarters of the students are attending classes with a view to improving their earning capacity and vocational competence; even though this type of education attracts participants of relatively high socio-economic status, which Johnstone's study indicates is the most strongly oriented toward non-vocational uses of education of any group in our population. That the decline in over-all rates of participation may be a consequence of the vocational preoccupation of university programing rather than a lack of potential relevance of non-vocational education for the older adult is suggested by Peers in a comparison of American and English university sponsored adult education programs.

> When we look a little more closely at the kind of work undertaken in university extension courses, the departure from the English model becomes clear. The programmes are, to an overwhelming extent concerned with courses which either provide 'credits' toward degrees, at both college and graduate levels, or are designed to increase professional qualifications. . . . While there are notable examples of more liberally conceived courses, university extension services, both through classes and through correspondence, are largely a projection of university degree credit programmes. . . . The tendency is, of course, for the universities to concentrate on those outside activities which pay their way, including not merely extension courses in subjects of professional interest, but also conferences and institutes which have been successful and tend to be repeated year after year (Peers, 1958, pp. 270-71).

He notes that this type of programing is aimed primarily at the younger adult of an above average income group and states that: "university extension activities of the American universities are . . . unlikely at present to contribute to a dynamic movement for liberal adult education" (ibid., p. 272). Finally his data show that in non-vocational and essentially "liberal education" offerings for adults—which constitute the bulk of university related adult education programs in England—the adults in the 40-60 year age range participate in numbers greater than would be indicated by their proportion of the total population, and the adults in the 60-75 age range are only slightly underrepresented; both of these figures being in sharp contrast to the American experience (Table 5).

Shifting Perceptions of the Relevance of Adult Education in the Later Stages of the Life Cycle: A Case Study

The English experience with non-vocational education for adults is not strictly comparable with the American in that it grew out of a different tradition, has had extensive government support, and is actively promoted by voluntary organizations as well as by the universities themselves. Our interest in the data is to formulate a case—i.e., the determining of participation potentials which might actually be achieved under appropriate conditions. Discussion indicated that part of the reason for the underrep-

TABLE 5

PERCENTAGE AGE DISTRIBUTION OF EAST MIDLAND ADULT
STUDENTS (1954-55) COMPARED WITH AGE DISTRIBUTION
OF ADULT POPULATION (ENGLAND, 1953)

Age-Group	Home Population Age 20 and Over	Sample of Adult Students	Adult Students Plus or Minus
20-29	19.9	17.2	-2.7
30-39	21.4	21.2	-0.2
40-49	22.2	25.4	+3.2
50-59	18.2	20.4	+2.2
60 and over (to 75 for home population)	18.3	13.7	-4.6

Source: Robert Peers, Adult Education: A Comparative Study,
London: Routledge & Kegan Paul, 1958, p. 179.

resentation of non-vocational and liberal education in university extension, and the consequent fall-off in participation of the middle aged and
older adult might stem from the commitment of the American university
to the vocationally oriented goals appropriate to the career development
phases of adult life. American society has been traditionally a work-ori-
ented society and participation in formal education may be accepted
most readily by the American adult in terms of the future time and instrumental value orientations that have characterized his earlier educational experiences. Similarly, the post-work and post-child rearing
phases of the life cycle have only recently emerged as stages of relatively long duration in the adult life cycle in which the work and family
goals are no longer dominant.

The problem confronting the adult educator in meeting the needs of
this phase of the life cycle, then, is not only one of changing his institutional commitment to one more appropriate to this form of non-vocational education, but also that of developing an awareness on the part of
the American adult of its significance. Some insights into changes in perceptions of liberal education which can occur in this phase of the life cycle can be gleaned from a study of a small group of participants in a four-
week adult residential seminar held at the University of Wisconsin. The
seminar was built around an integrated survey of the relationships between scientific and humanistic thought as they have developed over the

past four centuries in the Western World. It was primarily intended for alumni, but was open to the public. Although no mention was made of its appropriateness for the older adult, it was felt that persons would be attracted who are presently stressing leisure rather than work objectives in the pattern of life organization.

Of the group of 40 that enrolled, more than half were over 50 years old, only 5 were under 35. There was a 3 to 2 ratio of females to males. The numbers involved are too small to justify generalizations, but some observations can be made of possible interest to adult educators:

Reported Reasons for Enrollment—only two members of the group felt that participating would have any relation to work career; the rest voiced non-vocational ends for participation, stating them in rather vague and general terms of unspecified "needs" or interests in pursuing this type of educational interest further; a few responded to the nostalgic appeal for the return of the old grad which was contained in the literature; and one man came against his better judgment at the insistence of his wife.

Stage of Life Cycle—three of the group were retired and three were in semi-retirement; only four persons were in relatively early stages of their work career, and these were single women; the rest, although still active in their work or family careers, felt that their period of major family or work responsibility would be soon terminating and new patterns of life participation and satisfactions would be needed to replace the old; for the married women this meant that their children were about ready to leave home or had reached their teens and, in the fashion of today's adolescent, had convinced their parents that their period of dependency was about over and that the parent had better find new patterns of interest; for the men this meant that they were far enough along in their career lines for their period of upward striving to be past and were searching for challenges in addition to that of the job; significantly, most of the participants were undergoing a major change in their conception of self, having but recently realized the necessity for a major reorientation in life patterns and a redefinition of life goals; most were preparing for a period of life in which leisure rather than work was to be the dominant theme.

Previous Participation in Liberal Adult Education—contrary to our expectations only seven had had any extensive experience with formal programs of liberal adult education (and three of these were the younger single women of the group); these were not the "professional" participants in liberal education that the adult educator in this field is sometimes accused of catering to; most however had maintained an interest in liberal education during their adult life, pursuing it through private reading and discussion.

Expectations of the Program—for most of the participants this was a new and somewhat strange experience; many seemed puzzled and uneasy about being there, not sure that this would be an appropriate form of activity for them; during the entry interviews they expressed a fear that the others of the group would be "all women" or "mostly school teachers" (neither assumption proved to be correct); the man who came at his wife's insistence was frankly concerned as to what his fellow office workers would say about his spending vacation time in this manner instead of going fishing as originally planned; among those for whom participation represented a long deferred desire, a degree of perplexity existed as to why a university would be interested in structuring a program for persons well past the undergraduate student age. Terminal interviews revealed a major revision of original expectations for most; reassurance gained as to the appropriateness of this form of participation for them was reflected in such comments as "the group was much different than I expected, they were people just like me" (i.e., married couples, non-teachers, businessmen, engineers, as the case may be), "why hasn't this been done before," or "this is just what I've been hoping for"; perhaps the most drastic contrasts to original expectations were revealed in the remarks of the thwarted fisherman who became the program's most enthusiastic advocate; he not only gave an unqualified statement of the value of liberal adult education but also reported, in a tone of pleasant surprise, that the program had made him feel "old" for the first time, and added by way of explanation that he now realized that he needed to find life goals and interests beyond the immediate ones of job success and family-rearing.

This study helps to illustrate the reality of the newly emerged span of years in the life of adults during which the traditional interests of work and family are no longer sufficient organizing principles for a pattern of life activity, and indicates a possible relevance for the pursuits of liberal education to this new leisure class. The group studied was small and certainly typical in that they were mostly college graduates. Even among this highly select group, however, we found an initial doubt as to the appropriateness of this type of educational participation.

The significance of participation for this group has been threefold. First, it has restimulated a desire for systematic development of competence in an area which has long been of interest to them. The desire for planned reading and further course participation was expressed by nearly all of them. Second, it has helped to furnish a much needed sanction for such participating on the part of these older adults. And, finally, it seems to have helped them to identify an interest pattern particularly adapted to the leisure phase of the life cycle.

AMERICA'S ADULTS IN THE 'SIXTIES: THE DEMOGRAPHIC PICTURE

Henry D. Sheldon
Bureau of the Census

Any discussion of adults in the '60's involves a commitment as to who adults really are, and some elaboration of Mort Sahl's incontrovertable dictum that the future lies ahead.

I have settled the first of these issues by defining the adult population, somewhat arbitrarily, as the population 25 years old and over. The age group 18 to 24 is essentially a group in transition from childhood to adulthood. It is in this age range that a majority of children leave their parental home, complete their education, if female get married, are most mobile, and make preliminary adjustments in the labor market. By age 25, a majority of the population may be considered as having achieved adult status and some modicum of what might be considered adult stability.

I have further assumed that human beings in a given society, 'ike the mud wasp, have a life cycle. Although obviously not universally applicable, it is apparent that a majority of adults in a given age range are the parents of pre-school children, at a higher age level are the parents of teenagers, and pass progressively, as age increases, through a period in wh'ch the children have left home, a period of retirement, and a final period in which they survive their marriage partner. Dr. Paul Glick, one of my colleagues at the Bureau of the Census, has made a systematic formulation of this notion in various articles on the family cycle.[1] Cycles of this type, in the absence of catastrophic events, would appear to have in some measure a timeless Platonic quality which is a necessary by-product of biology and aging. To be sure, the modal age periods for each phase may change through time (and Dr. Glick has shown that they do), but they still exist.

---

1. See Paul C. Glick, David M. Heer, and John C. Beresford, "Family Formation and Family Composition," in Marvin B. Sussman: Source Book in Marriage and the Family (Boston: Houghton Mifflin Company), 1963 (2nd ed.).

At the same time, each generation or cohort may have unique characteristics which grow out of the dominant events of the period in which they become adults. These differences, or at least the most interesting ones, are apt to be in the field of attitudes and values, and thus not reflected in census statistics; there are, however, points at which this interpretation appears applicable. In the larger context it would be interesting to contrast the generation which became adult during the "Jazz Age," that is, those who were 15 to 24 in 1920 and 25 to 34 in 1930, with a similar group who moved from 15 to 24 to 25 to 34 in the depression decade.

In view of these considerations, data on the adult population are presented here in five age groups—10-year intervals from 25 to 64, and a final 65 and over group. The use of 10-year intervals obscures some interesting details. On the other hand, in view of the variety of subjects covered, a systematic presentation seems in order.

The second issue, that relating to future trends, presents a number of difficulties. There is a legend that an English economist, writing during World War II or somewhat thereafter, explored an analogy between the haruspex of ancient Rome, who predicted future events from an examination of the entrails of sacrificial sheep, and the modern statistician who specialized in projections. Both, he concluded, served a useful function in providing administrators with a credible basis for the determination of policy, but the relations between their predictions and future events were equally coincidental. This is perhaps an overstatement of the case, but the record of the accuracy of population projections has not been impressive although perhaps not much different from the prediction of the outcome of elections, future trends in security prices, or long-range weather forecasting. Although it is possible to simulate with considerable sophistication the processes by which population grows or declines, it is necessary, to get this machinery in motion, to make some assumptions concerning future trends in the number of births.

The use of electronic computers in population projections has vastly increased the range of experimentation with alternative methods and assumptions; and Whelpton's concept of cohort fertility which bases the estimates of the number of births to cohorts of women who have not completed their child bearing period on their past performance reduces to some degree the area of guesswork.[2] Even given improved population projections there is still the problem, if they are to be extended to other areas, of determining what the future trends in, for example, age-specific marriage rates or labor force participation rates are going to be. In short, although it is of great interest to speculate about the future it should be clear that it is speculation and not a "scientific" projection. Such remarks as I make concerning future trends clearly represent such speculation, based on varying degrees of information from subject to subject.

One other aspect of concern with the future has to do with those consumers of statistics who hold that, unless the statistics are as of tomorrow morning, they are utterly worthless. In the case of a highly volatile area such as unemployment, there is some basis for this position. Statistics on unemployment are highly perishable, and it is quite possible that some of the detailed cross-classifications of data on unemployment published from the 1960 census are of more historical than current interest. On the other hand, data on age structure, marital status, and many other subjects, are relatively inert to the degree that the data from one census serves as a reasonably good projection of the results observed in the succeeding census. It is in areas of this type that speculation as to the future would seem most reasonable—and least interesting.

Age Structure

Table 1 compares the age structure of the population 25 years old and over according to the 1960 census with that shown by the current projection for 1970. Since all that is involved is aging the population 15 years old and over in 1960 and making appropriate allowances for net immigration, many of the strictures mentioned in connection with population projections generally do not apply. Only if we were to enter into a period of unparalleled prosperity and Congress were to lift all restrictions on immigration, or if our population became infected with a deadly virus brought back from outer space by astronauts, would the 1970 figures be seriously out of line.

It will be noted that age group 25 to 34 in 1960 is smaller by about one million persons than the next older age group, and as this cohort ages

---

2. P. K. Whelpton, Cohort Fertility: Native White Women in the United States (Princeton: Princeton University Press), 1954.

TABLE 1

AGE AND SEX OF THE POPULATION 25 YEARS OLD AND OVER FOR THE UNITED STATES, 1960 WITH PROJECTION FOR 1970

(In thousands; includes Armed Forces overseas)

Year and Age	Total	Male	Female	Per Cent Distribution			Per Cent of Total	
				Total	Male	Female	Male	Female
1960 Census								
Total	99,710	48,321	51,389	100.0	100.0	100.0	48.5	51.5
25 to 34 years	22,996	11,369	11,627	23.1	23.5	22.6	49.4	50.6
35 to 44 years	24,158	11,845	12,313	24.2	24.5	24.0	49.0	51.0
45 to 54 years	20,640	10,175	10,465	20.7	21.1	20.4	49.3	50.7
55 to 64 years	15,709	7,600	8,109	15.8	15.7	15.8	48.4	51.6
65 years and over	16,207	7,332	8,875	16.3	15.2	17.3	45.2	54.8
1970 Projection								
Total	110,466	52,824	57,642	100.0	100.0	100.0	47.8	52.2
25 to 34 years	25,048	12,464	12,584	22.7	23.6	21.8	49.8	50.2
35 to 44 years	23,118	11,389	11,729	20.9	21.6	20.3	49.3	50.7
45 to 54 years	23,541	11,419	12,122	21.3	21.6	21.0	48.5	51.5
55 to 64 years	18,724	8,909	9,815	17.0	16.9	17.0	47.6	52.4
65 years and over	20,035	8,643	11,392	18.1	16.4	19.8	43.1	56.9

Source: U.S. Bureau of the Census, U.S. Census of Population: 1960, Vol. I, Part I, Tables 45 and 65; and Current Population Reports, Series P-25, No. 251.

through the decade to 1970 it is still smaller than either adjacent age group. This situation reflects in part the effects of the relatively small number of births during the depression decade, 1930-40. Actually, the age intervals chosen serve to obscure this effect. Persons born between 1930 and 1940 fell in the age group 20 to 29 in 1960. The number of persons in this group—about 22 million—was about 8 million smaller than the number 10 to 19, and 2 million smaller than the number 30 to 39. When the depression cohort becomes 30 to 39 in 1970, the projections tell us, this deficit will not change materially. In short, then, the age structure tends to reflect past trends in the numbers of births. In this connection, it may be worth noting that the increase in the population 65 years old and over between 1960 and 1970, although in part a reflection of improved mortality conditions, also reflects the fact that there were about 52 million births between 1870 and 1895, but 57 million between 1880 and 1905. The population 65 and over in 1970 represents the survivors of a larger birth cohort.

A comparison of the 1960 and 1970 age distributions of the adult population would seem to illustrate the inertia previously noted of certain population characteristics. Certainly this population will be older in 1970 than in 1960, but not much older: the per cent 45 and over will increase from 53 to 56 per cent and the per cent 65 and over from 16 to 18 per cent. Certainly an increase of 4 million in this older population is of considerable significance to persons planning or administering programs for older persons, but it is doubtful whether a casual observer could detect any differences between adult populations with a two per cent difference in the proportion of older persons.

Sex Composition

The figures in Table 1 suggest that in the adult population of 1960 there were more women than men, that the degree to which women outnumber men increases with age, and that these tendencies will increase during the present decade. The ratio between male and female birth is relatively constant and biased in favor of males. The mortality of males is, however, uniformly higher than for females, so that as age increases, the number of women relative to the number of men increases. Here again, however, the change is not cataclysmic—the figures suggest that in 1970 there will be 2 less men per 100 women than there were in 1960 —that is, the sex ratio will drop from 94 to 92.

69

Race and Nativity

Between 1900 and 1914 about 13 million immigrants entered this country. During World War I immigration fell off and, in the decade 1920-29, the number was 4.3 million reflecting, in part, the effects of the quota system established by the Immigration Act of 1924. During the depression years and World War II, there was little immigration—in fact, in many years a net emmigration. Since the late 40's, under the quota system, immigration has stabilized at between 2 and 3 million per decade. The net effect of this sequence of events has been to reduce the size of the foreign-born population from its 1930 peak. In 1930, the two largest age groups were 25 to 34 and 35 to 44, and their size (2.4 and 3.5 million respectively) gives a rough measure of the net effects of the heavy post- and pre-World War I immigration. By 1960 these cohorts were 55 to 64 and 65 to 74, respectively, and their predominant size is still reflected in census data. As these generations, or cohorts, reach the upper age brackets, they are subject to heavy mortality. The rough projection for 1970 suggests that most of the survivors of the heavy immigration in the first part of this century will be in the age group 65 and over and that, by 1980, will have in large part disappeared. Thus, in one sense, the objectives of the proponents of immigration restriction are being realized.

Apart from the decline in the proportion of the foreign-born white, there would appear to be little change in the nativity and racial composition of the population 25 years old and over. Both the native white and the nonwhite will show compensatory increases in percentage of the total but they will not be phenomenal. In general, then, in the adult population in 1970, about 10 persons out of 100 will be nonwhite; 7, foreign-born white; and the remaining 83, native white. Again, it would appear that such changes as do occur will not be apparent to the casual observer.

Geographic Distribution of Population

Between 1950 and 1960 there was a substantial net in-migration to the West, an out-migration from the South, a small outmovement from the North Central States, and a small movement into the Northeast (Table 2). It is obvious that the regional figures do not necessarily represent the trends in their various parts. Although a majority of the states in the South lost population through migration, Florida gained about 1.5

TABLE 2

NET MIGRATION 1950 TO 1960 AND 1940 TO 1950 BY METROPOLITAN
STATUS, COLOR AND REGION, FOR THE UNITED STATES
(In thousands)

Region, Metropolitan-Nonmetropolitan Residence and Color	1960	1950	Net Change 1950-60		Components of Change			Net Total Migration 1940-1950
			Amount	Rate	Natural Increase	Net Total Migration		
						Amount	Rate	
Total								
United States	179,323	151,326	+27,997	+18.5	25,337	+2,660	+ 1.8	+1,362
Northeast	44,678	39,478	+ 5,200	+13.2	4,864	+ 336	+ 0.9	+ 310
North Central	51,619	44,461	+ 7,158	+16.1	7,280	- 121	- 0.3	- 316
South	54,973	47,197	+ 7,776	+16.5	9,180	-1,404	- 3.0	-2,135
West	28,053	20,190	+ 7,863	+38.9	4,013	+3,850	+19.1	+3,503
Nonwhite								
United States	20,491	16,176	+ 4,315	+26.7	4,341	- 25	+ 0.2	- 160
Northeast	3,155	2,079	+ 1,076	+51.8	535	+ 541	+26.0	+ 483
North Central	3,616	2,341	+ 1,275	+54.5	717	+ 558	+23.8	+ 632
South	11,496	10,348	+ 1,148	+11.1	2,606	-1,457	-14.1	-1,597
West	2,223	1,408	+ 815	+57.9	483	+ 332	+23.6	+ 323
Metropolitan State Economic Areas								
United States	111,359	88,110	+23,249	+26.4	15,107	+8,143	+ 9.2	+7,218
Northeast	36,050	31,847	+ 4,203	+13.2	3,895	+ 309	+ 1.0	+ 411
North Central	30,090	24,324	+ 5,766	+23.7	4,486	+1,281	+ 5.3	+1,273
South	25,431	18,622	+ 6,809	+36.6	4,090	+2,719	+14.6	+2,356
West	19,787	13,316	+ 6,471	+48.6	2,637	+3,834	+28.8	+3,177
Nonmetropolitan State Economic Areas								
United States	67,964	63,216	+ 4,748	+ 7.5	10,231	-5,483	- 8.7	-5,923
Northeast	8,627	7,631	+ 996	+13.1	969	+ 27	+ 0.4	- 42
North Central	21,529	20,137	+ 1,392	+ 6.9	2,794	-1,402	- 7.0	-1,606
South	29,542	28,575	+ 967	+ 3.4	5,091	-4,124	-14.4	-4,598
West	8,266	6,874	+ 1,392	+20.3	1,377	+ 16	+ 0.2	+ 323

Source: U.S. Bureau of the Census, U.S. Census of Population: 1960, Vol. I, Part 1,
Table 9; and Current Population Reports, Series P-23, No. 7 and P-25, No. 247.

million and there were substantial gains in the states in the national Capitol area and appreciable gains in Texas. In the West, the gains were heavily concentrated in California, Arizona, and Colorado, although all of the states except Montana, Idaho, and Wyoming showed some gain. The industrial states of the North Central region—Ohio, Michigan, Illinois, and Indiana have appreciable gains from migration although over-all the region showed a slight loss. In the Northeast, the gains were concentrated in Connecticut, New York, and New Jersey.

If there is any descriptive general formula, it would be that the movement of population was out of the "heartland" and to the periphery—California and the Southwest, the Gulf Coast, Florida, the East Coast metropolitan region (beginning with the national Capitol area and ending with Boston), and the industrial Great Lake states. These generalizations, of course, are based on figures relating to the total rather than the adult population. It is an open question whether or not this pattern of movement will continue during the present decade. Since, with some variation, the same pattern occurred in the decade 1940-50, the easy answer is an affirmative one. There is some indication, however, from the current state estimates program that some of these streams of migration are slackening. Generally this is an area in which the fallibility of projections has frequently been demonstrated.

Movement of Nonwhite Population

As the figures in Table 2 indicate, the decade 1950-60 was marked by a heavy nonwhite outmigration from the South. In fact, there is some evidence that white population of the South gained from migration during the decade. This movement has been typically to the industrialized metropolitan areas of other regions of the country. During the decade, the nonwhite population of standard metropolitan statistical areas (SMSA's) outside the South increased by nearly 60 per cent, from about 5 to 8 million, and in 1960 the New York SMSA had a larger Negro population than any southern state. The movement of nonwhite population out of the South has gone on for a number of decades; the conservative prediction would be that it will continue in the present decade. Such a prediction may be wrong, but it would take considerable ingenuity and an imposing array of evidence to support a contrary hypothesis.

Movement into Metropolitan Areas

The movement of nonwhites into metropolitan areas is but a special case of a general movement involving the entire population. As Table 2 indicates, there was a net in-migration of about eight million persons to metropolitan state economic areas during the past decade; increases of this type occurred in all regions of the country. In terms of population change, generally about 85 per cent of the total increase in the country occurred in SMSA's, and the comparable figure for the decade 1940-50 was about 80 per cent. Over-all, the rate of increase between 1950 and 1960 in SMSA's was about 26 per cent as compared with 19 per cent for the country as a whole. Only in the Northeast did it fall below the national level and in the rapidly growing West it was nearly 50 per cent.

Given, first, the current definition of SMSA's which begins with a city of 50,000 or more (and which therefore tends to pick up and classify as metropolitan the most rapidly-growing urban centers); second, the fact that ours is an essentially urban industrial economy; and third, the declining need for agricultural manpower, it seems highly probable that the concentration of population in metropolitan areas will continue to increase.

Central City vs. Suburb

The consideration of differences between metropolitan and nonmetropolitan areas raises the further question as to differences within metropolitan areas—between the inhabitants of the central city and those of the remainder of the metropolitan area, the periphery or ring. During the past decade this area, usually described as suburban, has attracted a great deal of attention. There have been television specials celebrating the suburbs in song and dance; it is one of the favorite locales for television beer commercials; William Whyte has discussed the mass-produced suburbs in the Organization Man; there have been popular articles on the harried suburban wife and mother; on the suburb in politics; and there is even a developing school of sociology which maintains that careful analysis shows that suburbs do not exist.

The 1960 census has also made a contribution to the literature on suburbs. If the population of central cities is regarded as the "city" population and the population of the remainder of SMSA's is regarded as "suburban," then the 1960 figures showed that suburban areas were the areas of most rapid population growth during the decade. The population of central cities increased by about 11 per cent whereas the metropolitan area outside central cities increased by 49 per cent; or, if the area annexed to central cities during the decade is regarded as essentially suburban, the central cities gained by only about two per cent and the ring by 62 per cent. In terms of 1960 city limits, something more than one-fourth of the central cities lost population and, of the five cities of 1,000,000 or more—New York, Chicago, Los Angeles, Philadelphia, and Detroit—only one, Los Angeles, had an increase; all of the others lost population. At the other extreme in central cities with extremely high rates of growth during the decade, such as Tucson and Phoenix, a majority of the 1960 population lived in areas annexed since 1950. As noted earlier in this discussion, SMSA's accounted for more than four-fifths of the growth of total population during the decade, and of this growth about three-quarters occurred in the metropolitan area outside central cities.

If the decade growth in total population was heavily concentrated in the metropolitan area outside central cities and, as statistics on migration suggest, young adults are the most frequent movers, then it seems reasonable to expect that young adults will be over-represented in the ring population and under-represented in the central city population. The data in Table 3 confirm this expectation to a limited degree. This same

TABLE 3

PER CENT DISTRIBUTION BY RELATIONSHIP AND FAMILY STATUS OF THE POPULATION 25 YEARS OLD AND OVER BY AGE, FOR CONTERMINOUS UNITED STATES: 1960 AND 1950

Relationship and Family Status	Total	25 to 34 Years	35 to 44 Years	45 to 54 Years	55 to 64 Years	65 Years and Over
1960						
All persons	100.0	100.0	100.0	100.0	100.0	100.0
In primary families	88.0	92.9	93.7	90.7	84.2	72.9
Heads in husband-wife families	37.7	36.9	40.9	40.9	38.2	29.5
Wives in husband-wife families	35.6	41.3	41.9	38.2	32.0	18.5
Other male heads	1.2	0.6	0.9	1.3	1.5	2.2
Female heads	4.0	2.5	3.6	4.3	4.7	6.0
Other relatives	9.5	11.6	6.5	6.0	7.9	16.8
Unrelated individuals	10.5	6.1	5.3	8.2	14.4	23.3
Primary individuals	7.7	2.8	3.2	5.9	11.4	19.7
Secondary individuals[1]	2.8	3.3	2.1	2.3	3.0	3.5
Under care in institutions	1.5	1.0	0.9	1.1	1.4	3.8
1950						
All persons	100.0	100.0	100.0	100.0	100.0	100.0
In primary families	87.5	91.3	91.6	88.5	84.2	75.6
Heads in husband-wife families	35.4	33.0	38.7	38.9	37.3	27.4
Wives in husband-wife families	33.9	38.5	39.5	36.2	30.0	16.5
Other male heads	1.5	0.6	1.0	1.6	2.1	3.3
Female heads	3.8	1.5	2.9	4.4	5.6	7.3
Other relatives	12.9	17.7	9.5	7.4	9.2	21.1
Unrelated individuals	11.1	7.8	7.4	10.3	14.3	21.4
Primary individuals	5.2	1.6	2.6	4.8	8.0	14.4
Secondary individuals[1]	5.8	6.1	4.8	5.5	6.3	6.9
Under care in institutions	1.4	0.9	1.0	1.2	1.5	3.1

[1]Includes the relatively small number of persons in secondary families.

Source: U.S. Bureau of the Census, U.S. Census of Population: 1960, Vol. I, Part 1, Tables 183 and 184, and U.S. Census of Population: 1950, Vol. IV, Part 2, Chapter D, Table 1.

modest difference also appears in connection with other characteristics associated with the suburban image. In the aggregate, median income, median educational attainment, and the per cent in professional and managerial occupations are slightly higher for the ring than for the central cities. An examination of individual SMSA's shows that some conform to this image and some do not—and it is the examination of the latter group which has led certain sociologists to relegate the upper middle class suburb to the realm of myth and legend.

The problem is one of a more precise agreement as to what constitutes a suburb. Implicitly, the foregoing discussion assumes all the metropolitan area outside central cities is suburban area. Since, outside New England, SMSA's are made up of whole counties, the make-up of this territory is heterogeneous. For example, the rings of the Detroit and Chicago SMSA's include such relatively large cities as Pontiac, Dearborn, Evanston, Oak Park, and Cicero. At the other extreme, the San Bernardino-Riverside-Ontario SMSA contains such exotic suburbs as Cucumonga of burlesque skit fame, Twentynine Palms, and Palm Springs, as well as some 25,000 square miles of desert. In writing an article on suburban living it is possible to pick from this variety examples which are congruent with the particular theme to be developed. The Bureau of the Census, in contrast, has the responsibility of putting every last inhabitant into some category with the result that the variety tends to average out toward dead center.

One distinction which may be helpful in attempting to identify the true suburban population is a distinction between old and new suburbs. Forest Park, Illinois, a suburb of Chicago, first appeared in the census of 1880 with a population of 923. By 1930 it had attained a population of about 15,000, and the total population has remained relatively constant at this level to the present time. The median age of the population in 1960 was 35.4 years, 13 per cent of the population was 65 and over, 25 per cent 25 to 44, and 16 per cent under 10. This place might serve as an example of an old suburb. In contrast there is Park Forest, and the reversal in word order indicates its newness. This Chicago suburb was mass-produced shortly after the end of World War II; in 1950 it had a population of about 8,000 and by 1960 it had reached the 30,000 level. Here the median age of the population was 21.4 years, about 2 per cent of the population was 65 and over, 38 per cent 25 to 44, and 36 per cent under 10.

In this example it so happens that the median family income, median years of school completed, the percentage of the employed in white collar occupations, and the cumulative fertility rate for Park Forest are all higher than the corresponding indexes for Forest Park. It does not necessarily follow that this pattern of difference between old and new suburbs is universal. Oak Park, for example, which certainly qualifies as an old suburb, had in 1960 a higher median family income than Park Forest. Some moderate correlation would be expected, however, since generally income, educational attainment, and percentage of white collar workers are higher among adults under 45, than among adults 45 and over. Park Forest is by no means a unique phenomenon. An examination of the age tables for urban places in metropolitan areas indicate a fair number of places in which there was an age distribution similar to that of Park Forest, and in which further investigation would show a reasonable conformity to the stereotype of a suburb.

Another source of hidden suburban population lies in the areas annexed to cities during the past decade. In the El Paso SMSA for example, the contrast in terms of economic indexes places the population of higher socio-economic status within the central city. If, however, the census tracts entirely within the area annexed during the past decade (it had a population of more than 125,000 in 1960) are examined, a majority appear to exhibit the characteristic traits of new suburbs. This phenomena is obviously not confined to El Paso. Nor are annexations necessarily required —if far-seeing city fathers have in the past extended city limits well beyond the area of settlement and new residential section has been established in the vacant area, it is reasonable to assume that the inhabitants will have the characteristic suburban stigmata. Populations of this type are also found in the built-up unincorporated areas in the ring, but such populations are not readily identifiable in the census statistics.

If we define the suburban population as the population of young adults and their families living in relatively new housing on the periphery of urban agglomerations, then it is clear that such a population does exist and, could the various segments be readily assembled, might stand in dramatic contrast to the remaining population of metropolitan areas. Its size would certainly be less than that indicated for the ring of metropolitan areas as indicated in Table 3.

Whether or not the population of the ring in general will continue to grow at the expense of the central city is an open question. If the population as a whole continues to grow I would expect the population of central cities, except for annexation, to stabilize around present levels and the growth to occur in the ring. I am not impressed with the argument that urban renewal and similar measures are about to halt and reverse the flight to the suburbs. Although I certainly am not qualified to make this judgment, it seems to me that in the end the greater relative ease of bulldozing additional farm land and mass-producing split-levels will win out in the end. To be sure, there is a considerable movement from ring to central city, but in the long run the net is likely to be outward.

To cloud further the crystal ball, it is conceivable that the distinction between city and suburb may be on the verge of declining in importance. In a number of metropolitan areas, there have been movements to supplant, or at least supplement, municipal government with metropolitan government, and, in one or two instances, these proposals have been put into effect. For example, by a special election in 1962 a charter was established for the Metropolitan Government of Nashville and Davidson County by which the city of Nashville is downgraded to an "Urban Service District." Similarly, in the Norfolk area there have been recent instances of independent cities annexing whole counties. If these instances can be regarded as the beginning of a trend, it may be that the significance of the central city-ring classification will gradually decline. In view of the vested interests in the status quo, however, it does seem to me that the diffusion of such innovations will be slow.

Educational Attainment

Census figures indicate that educational attainment declines with age in the adult population. Among persons 25 to 34 only 10 per cent have completed less than eight years of elementary school, but among persons 65 and over the corresponding percentage was 42, and an examination of the percentages of those who had completed one or more years of college indicates the expected downward trend.

Although some persons may acquire additional education after 25 years of age, the number is not great enough to have any appreciable effect on the mass statistics. Thus each age group reflects the accessibility of education in the decade in which the group aged from 15 to 24 years to 25 to 34 years. For example, the cohort which was 55 to 64 in 1960 completed their education in the decade 1920-30; their educational level reflects the availability of education in that decade. Since the availability of education has steadily increased as well as the inclination on the part of the general population to take advantage of this opportunity, the educational level of each succeeding younger cohort has increased.

According to this logic, the cohort becoming 25 to 34 in 1970 will have a higher attainment level than the one which became 25 to 34 in 1960. This is not only a matter of applying past performance to the future but, more concretely, the Sputnik-inspired renaissance in education as well as the effort to deal with the drop-out problem should be reflected in the 1970 figures. At the same time, mortality will make heavy inroads at the upper levels at which the lowest attainment levels exist. The net effect should be for the adult population as a whole, that the level of educational attainment will rise during the decade.

Labor Force Participation

As census data indicate, the proportion of men 25 years old and over in the work force in 1960 was slightly less than in 1950. The participation rates between the ages of 25 and 54 in 1960, however, were slightly higher than the corresponding rates in 1950, whereas at 55 and above, the 1960 rates were lower—notably for men 65 and over. This downward movement of the labor force participation rates among older men represents the continuation of a long-time downward trend which was interrupted only briefly during the peak years of industrial effort during World War II. Between 1890 and 1940, the rate dropped from an estimated 68 per cent for men 65 and over, to 42. In 1945, it was 49, but by 1950 had dropped back to the 1940 level. The reasons for this decline are complex.

It can and has been argued that the drop reflects the increasing rate of technological changes and therefore the increasing rate of obsolescence of occupational skills. This explanation fits neatly into current concern with the effect of automation and the retraining program. Other factors which have been considered are the decline in self-employment and in agricultural employment (which turn out to be overlapping to a large extent), and the increasing life span which increases the numbers at the extreme upper age range who are unable to work. On the supply side of the equation, it should be noted that the social security system provides retirement income to a large segment of the older population who, prior to the establishment of this system, had little or no income other than that from employment.

Among women, the labor force participation rates showed an appreciable increase between 1950 and 1960, and again, this represents a continuation of a reasonably long time trend. Generally, the rates for women

78

show two peaks—one at 20 to 24 and the other in the middle years. The first of these peaks represents the high level of employment immediately prior to marriage and in the early years of marriage, and the second arises at the point at which the decline in family responsibilities makes feasible continued absence from the home during the day—usually the point at which all children are safely in school. This obviously is far from the entire explanation but, presumably, if a single event is to be mentioned, this is it. In 1960, the second peak in labor force participation occurred in the age group 45 to 54, and thereafter the rate declined. It is of interest to note however that, at the two upper age groups, the 1960 rates were higher than those for 1950, again indicating the general increase in labor force participation among women.

Women however seem to have a somewhat more tenuous connection with the labor force than men. At both ages 25 to 34 and 45 to 54 about 85 per cent of the men had worked 40 or more weeks in the previous year. For women this percentage was about 55 at ages 25 to 34, and 68 at ages 45 to 54. For men 25 to 54 the per cent working 13 weeks or less in the previous year ranged between one and three. For women the corresponding range was from 11 to 20 per cent. These figures suggest that the competition for women between employment and family responsibilities leads to considerably more movement in and out of the labor market than is characteristic of men.

Projections of labor force participation rates have not been notably successful. The cowardly way out is simply to say that, in the absence of evidence to the contrary, past trends will continue. By 1970, it will not be unreasonable to expect a further decline in the participation rate among older men and some increase in the rate for women of all ages.

Occupational Distribution

The occupational distribution presented in Table 4 is an adaptation and condensation of the standard census classification by major occupation group. The use of the census classification is obviously dictated by the use of census statistics; it has the virtue of being reasonably consistent from census to census and has a specifiable relationship to standard international classifications.

The percentage distribution by occupational groups reflects the operation of a variety of processes, and similar changes in proportions from

TABLE 4

PER CENT DISTRIBUTION OF THE EMPLOYED POPULATION 25 YEARS OLD
AND OVER, BY MAJOR OCCUPATION GROUP, AGE AND SEX, FOR
THE UNITED STATES: 1960
(Distributions based on total reporting occupation)

Sex and Occupation Group	1950 Total	1960					
		Total	25 to 34 Years	35 to 44 Years	45 to 54 Years	55 to 64 Years	65 Years and Over
Male, employed	100.0	100.0	100.0	100.0	100.0	100.0	100.0
Professional and managerial	20.2	23.9	24.3	24.9	23.5	22.2	23.2
Professional	8.0	11.4	15.5	12.0	9.1	7.9	8.8
Managerial	12.2	12.5	8.7	12.9	14.4	14.3	14.4
Clerical and sales	12.3	13.5	14.7	13.4	12.5	13.0	15.0
Craftsmen and operatives	39.3	41.7	43.9	44.3	42.6	38.4	24.7
Craftsmen	20.0	21.7	20.8	23.2	22.6	21.5	14.9
Operatives	19.4	20.1	23.1	21.1	20.0	16.9	9.9
Service workers[1]	6.2	6.2	4.9	4.9	6.2	8.5	11.5
Laborers[2]	7.5	6.3	6.6	5.9	6.3	6.6	6.0
Farm workers[3]	14.5	8.4	5.6	6.6	8.9	11.2	19.7
Female, employed	100.0	100.0	100.0	100.0	100.0	100.0	100.0
Professional and managerial	18.7	18.9	18.4	16.4	20.3	21.0	21.0
Professional	13.3	14.3	15.9	12.3	14.8	14.8	14.0
Managerial	5.4	4.6	2.5	4.1	5.5	6.2	7.0
Clerical and sales	31.9	36.8	41.6	38.8	35.6	32.1	24.6
Craftsmen and operatives	22.4	19.0	19.0	21.4	19.1	16.5	12.6
Craftsmen	1.7	1.4	1.1	1.5	1.5	1.5	1.3
Operatives	20.7	17.6	17.8	19.9	17.5	15.0	11.3
Service workers[1]	22.3	23.0	19.1	21.1	22.6	27.6	37.8
Laborers[2]	0.8	0.5	0.5	0.6	0.5	0.5	0.5
Farm workers[3]	3.7	1.9	1.4	1.7	1.9	2.3	3.6

[1] Includes private household workers.

[2] Excludes farm and mine workers.

[3] Includes farmers, farm managers, and farm laborers.

Source: U.S. Bureau of the Census, U.S. Census of Population: 1960, Vol. I, Part 1,
Table 204, and U.S. Census of Population: 1950, Vol. II, Part I, Table 127.

age group to age group may reflect the operation of quite different processes or combinations thereof. The appreciable drop, for example, among
male craftsmen and operatives at 65 and over reflects a higher rate of
retirement in these groups than in some of the other occupation groups.
The absence of this decline in the managerial and proprietary group and
among clerical and sales workers is, in all probability, evidence of a
lower retirement rate. The sharp increase in the proportion of farm workers, however, does not necessarily mean that "old farmers never die—
they just fade away" but that, like the foreign-born at 65 and over, they
are the last survivors of initially large cohorts going back to the period
when the requirements for agricultural manpower were considerably
greater. The same kind of distribution is evident in the detailed statistics
for such occupations as tailor and blacksmith. The similar increase

among service workers at the upper age levels does not reflect a contracting occupational group but accretion by downward occupational mobility from other occupational groups at the upper age levels.

Increases to the middle age ranges frequently reflect upward occupational mobility. In the present figures, this process is illustrated by the craftsmen and operative groups. The percentage of craftsmen increases between the age groups 25 to 34 and 35 to 44 and then remains at a relatively constant level through ages 55 to 64. Operatives, on the other hand, initially a larger percentage of the total at 25 to 34, show a continuous decline through the remainder of the age span. A part of the decline represents the shift of operatives into the craftsmen and foremen group. Similarly, the managerial and proprietary group represent occupations which require a background of training and experience and therefore are attained later in life. In contrast, entrance into the professional occupations is based primarily on training with the result that they are entered at the beginning of working life. The decline in the proportion of professional workers as age increases reflects the fact that this is an expanding occupational group. The larger numbers in the younger age groups reflect in large part the proliferation of professional occupations. The operation of this principle is illustrated by the fact that among aeronautical engineers only 16 per cent are 45 years old or over, whereas the corresponding figure for civil engineers is 38 per cent.

The occupational classification used permits the classification of the employed into three major divisions: first, the group normally designated as white collar workers—professional managerial, clerical, and sales workers; second, what roughly might be described as industrial workers —craftsmen and operatives; and a residual blue collar group—service workers, laborers, and farm workers. Among employed men 25 years old and over in 1960, the white collar group constituted a little less than 40 per cent of the total, the industrial group a little more than 40 per cent, and the residual other group about 20 per cent. The white collar group remained a relatively constant proportion of the total at all age levels; the proportion in the industrial group remained relatively constant to age 55 and then declined, and at this point there were compensatory gains in the residual other group.

Among employed women 25 and over in 1960, about 55 per cent were found in the white collar group, 20 per cent in the industrial group, and the remaining 25 per cent in the residual group. At the upper age levels, there were declines in both the white collar and industrial groups and compensating gains in the residual group.

The classification also provides the basis for a hierarchy in terms of income—the aggregate median earnings figures for professional and managerial male workers fell midway between $6,000 and $7,000,,for clerical and sales workers, between $4,500 and $5,000, for craftsmen between $5,000 and $5,500, and for operatives between $4,000 and $4,500. The medians for the remaining groups were all well under $4,000. The median earnings figures for women workers were considerably below those for men, reflecting the well known sex differential in wage and salary level and the irregular pattern of female labor force participation.

Income

Between 1949 and 1959 there was a substantial increase in income. In terms of purchasing power some part of this increase was illusory since in the same time period there was also an increase in consumer prices. In terms of constant dollars, however, there was still a net gain in real income. Estimates based on data from the Current Population Survey indicate that in terms of constant (1959) dollars, average family money income increased from about $4,000 in 1947 to $5,400 in 1959, a rise that averaged approximately $120 per year over this period.

The typical pattern by age—here again for both types of income and for men and unrelated individuals—is an increase between the age groups 25 to 34 and 35 to 44 and thereafter a decline which is particularly sharp at 65 and over. This pattern is characteristic of most occupation groups. The drop at ages 65 and over is probably universal. In the professional group as a whole the peak advances into the next age interval—45 to 54 years. For a few select groups such as college professors, civil engineers, economists, and social scientists the peak earning period is 55 to 64. Lest our hearts bleed excessively for the sad plight of the older middle-aged worker, it should be recognized that there are hazards involved in deducing life histories from cross sectional statistics by age. If we examine the statistics from a cohort perspective it is clear that among men, although those who became 35 to 44 in 1960 had the greatest decennial increase in median income, the two succeeding cohorts also had substantial

82

increases in median income in the 10-year period in which they attained the ages of 45 to 54 and 55 to 64 respectively. They may indeed, if they are aware of the statistics, be envious of their juniors for cornering a disproportionately large share of the proceeds from our affluent society, but they suffered no decline in money income.

More seriously, in order to establish an undated relationship between age and income it would be necessary to take a life history or cohort approach. If this were possible it would probably turn out that each cohort would have unique income history, so that a perfectly generalized statement of the relationship would still be difficult.

For the purpose of describing the adult population it may suffice to say that incomes on the average in 1960 were higher for the population 25 to 44 than they were for the population 45 and over. The income picture for women was considerably different than that for men. In the first place, excepting those 65 and over, more than 40 per cent reported no income. These women presumably are in large part those who are homemakers. In the second place, their average incomes are extremely low in comparison to those for men. As noted in the discussion of occupation, this difference is in part a function of the sex differentials in wage rate, and of the tenuous connection of women with the work force. To these factors might be added the fact that employed women tend to be concentrated in the occupation groups in which earnings are low.

Marital Status

There are three useful statistics in explaining sex and age differences in marital status. First, women live longer than men. In 1960 the expectation of life at birth for white females was 74.1 years—for males it was 67.4 years. Second, women on the average are younger at the time of marriage than men. Data from a recent Current Population Survey indicated that men, on the average, are about 2.5 years older than women on the date of first marriage. Earlier studies indicate that this difference increases with age and is higher for remarriages. Third, men at the upper age levels tend to remarry more frequently than women. Of the married men 65 and over in 1960 about 22 per cent were remarried; the corresponding figure for married women in the same age group was 17 per cent.

The difference in age at marriage explains why the greatest per cent married occurs in the age group 25 to 34 for women, but in the age group 35 to 44 for men. The differential mortality rate compounded by the age difference explains the more rapid decline with age in per cent married for women. The greater remarriage rate for men also contributes to this difference but it is particularly relevant to the fact that at 65 and over about 70 per cent of the men but only 37 per cent of the women are married. In popular articles the decline in the sex ratio is frequently viewed with alarm as a potential source of husband deprivation but actually in 1960 the proportion of married persons (that is, married, widowed and divorced) was greater among women than among men. Actually the excess women are those who have been through the marriage cycle—or, if you will, run through their husbands—and wind up, because of their earlier marriage and greater longevity, as elderly widows.

It will be noted that the percentage of single women (but not single men) increased from 55 to 64, and 65 and over in both 1950 and 1960. This appears to be a case of differential mortality. Although the death rate for single women is higher than that for married women, it is lower than that for widowed or divorced women. With the tremendous increase in widowhood at the upper age levels the death rates for single women become lower than those all other women, and thus single women become an increasing proportion of the total. In the interests of economy and space, the divorced have been combined with the widowed. Over-all they constituted in 1960 about two per cent of the male, and three per cent of the female, population 14 years old and over.

As in the case of income, it can be argued that a cohort rather than a cross sectional approach is needed and, as in the case of income, the use of the cross sectional approach may be misleading. If we examine the per cent married among women 25 to 34 and 35 to 44 in 1960 and find that this per cent dropped from 87.5 to 87.1, we may be led to infer that the inroads of male mortality are already in evidence. If however, we examine the 1960, 35 to 44 cohort in 1950 when it was 25 to 34 we find that the per cent married was only 84.7 and the per cent single was appreciably higher. We are thus led to the happy conclusion that at these ages, in the past decade, single women are still getting married. At the higher age levels when the decline in the per cent married has really started, the cross sectional figures yield the correct direction if not the exact magnitude.

In summary then, at ages under 45 more than four-fifths of the adult population was married in 1960. At the ages of 45 and over this percentage declined progressively, more rapidly for women than for men, and there were complementary increases in the per cent widowed and divorced. A comparison of the 1950 and 1960 figures suggests that the general improvement in mortality reduced in some measure the extent of this decline. If the improvement in mortality continues during this decade, and we have every reason to believe that it will, the extent of the decline in the per cent married will be further reduced.

Relationship and Family Status

In the census classification, a family is defined as a group of related persons living together. A primary family is one in which the family head is also the household head. There are also secondary families—families in which the head of the family is not the household head, as for example, a mother and child living as lodgers. The number of such families is small as is the number of persons in them, and in Table 3 they have been included with secondary individuals—the category covering lodgers, resident servants, and the like. Under age 55, 90 per cent or more of the population lived in primary families in 1960. At 55 and over, this proportion declined; this decline in large part reflected the decline in the proportion married just considered.

Unrelated individuals are persons who live in the absence of relatives. Generally if they live in a house or in an apartment they are dignified with the title of household head and are primary individuals; if on the other hand they live as lodgers in someone else's household they are secondary individuals. If they share their apartment with other persons unrelated to them, one member of such a partnership is designated as the head and becomes a primary individual and the other members of the group secondary individuals. The shift from secondary to primary individuals between 1950 and 1960 reflects to some degree a liberalization of the definition of what constitutes a dwelling or housing unit and thus an independent household. The change in definition was such that, had you lived in the YWCA in 1950, you would have been classified as a secondary individual but if you still lived there in 1960 you would have, in all probability, been classified as a primary individual.

As Table 3 indicates, the proportion of people living as unrelated individuals increases with age, particularly at 65 and over. This increase obviously complements the decrease in primary family members and represents a type of adjustment to family dissolution as the result of the death of a marriage partner. At 65 and over a relatively high proportion of the unrelated individuals are widows.

A comparison of the 1950 and the 1960 figures suggests some changes which are worthy of note. First there is the decline in the proportion at the upper age levels living as other relatives in primary families coupled with the increase in unrelated individuals at these ages. At this age level, parents of the family head or his wife constitute the major part of the "other relative" category. The shifts in proportions would suggest that in the event of widowhood in an elderly couple the widow is less likely to come to live with one of her children and more likely to be set up, or maintained, as an independent householder. The second change relates to the decline in the proportions of other relatives at younger ages and the similar decline in unrelated individuals. Fledglings who have not yet left the parental nest comprise a considerable element in the former group and young adults, more or less on the loose, a considerable element in the latter group. It seems likely that considerable numbers of both groups succumbed to the attraction of "togetherness" and married during the decade, and this accounts for the increases in the proportions of heads of husband-wife families and in wives.

Presence of Children

Since it is not an undue exaggeration to describe parenthood as a distinct way of life, no description of the adult population is complete without some reference to this phenomenon.

Of the 45 million families in the United States in 1960, about 40 million, or something slightly less than 90 per cent, were husband-wife families. The remaining families—those with other male heads and female heads—were, in terms of the age of the head, relatively older than husband-wife families, and a greater proportion of them were without children. As the data on relationship suggest, a majority of them represent families that have been broken by death or divorce.

Among husband-wife families in which the head was 35 to 44, 86 per cent had as members own children under 18 years old. This percentage split about evenly between families with children under six, and families with children six to 17 years old. For families in which the head was 65 and over, there were few with children under six, but nearly four per cent with school-age children. In one sense, it can be argued that these figures merely prove what everybody knows. On the other hand, there is some virtue in setting exact values to these bits of common knowledge.

Slightly more than 90 per cent of the families with their own children under six were families in which the head was under 45 years of age, and slightly less than 90 per cent of the families with children six to 17 were families in which the head was under 55. It seems not unreasonable to designate men between 25 and 44 as the parents of pre-school children, and, although there is a great deal of overlap, the age range 45 to 54 as the terminal phase of active parenthood. As Glick's studies have shown, the median ages at marriage, birth of first child, and median age of the parent when the last child leaves home, have declined during this century. There seems to be no compelling reason to doubt that these trends will continue into the 60's.

Adults in the 60's

In order to develop a more coherent picture of adults in the '60's, it may be desirable to consider this population in three age groups: those 25 to 44, those 45 to 64, and those 65 years old and over. The first of the periods, in contrast to the remaining two, might be designated as a period of greater activity both in intensity and variety. This group will be the most mobile, will have a larger proportion living in new suburbs, and will contain the highest proportion of college graduates. It will contain the highest proportion of men in the labor force, and will, in contrast to the other groups, be overrepresented in newer occupations. Its members will experience the most rapid rise in income. A larger proportion of its members will be married and the parents of pre-school children.

The second group will have reached a plateau with respect to activities. They will be less mobile; those who live in suburbs will live in suburbs that were new 20 years ago. The educational level of this group will not be as high as that of the younger group; their income will have increased less rapidly and, although some of the members will have moved upward into occupations which require greater skill and training, others will have reached a plateau while still others will be having difficulties in maintaining themselves in contracting occupations. The proportion married and members of primary families will decline slowly in this age period. Retirement from active parenthood for most persons will be completed in this period, and there will be an appreciable proportion retired from the labor force by the end of the period.

At 65 and over there will be further decline in mobility, educational level, and income, and increasing numbers of persons will retire from the labor force. The proportion of persons who are married, and who are members of primary families will decline. Women will comprise an increasing proportion of the group; a majority of them will be widows. This perhaps is too lugubrious a description of the situation of the older population but it is sufficiently real to be the basis for the current interest in, and programs for resolving, the problems of this population group.

If this summary overgeneralizes, omits relevant detail, and perverts a few facts, these are inevitable limitations incident to an attempt to distill a few pearls of wisdom from a mass of data on a phenomenon as varied and kaleidoscopic as the adult population of the United States.

ADULT USES OF EDUCATION: FACT AND FORECAST[*]

John W. C. Johnstone
University of Chicago

The purpose of this paper is to review the current educational practices of American adults. There are three main sections to the paper.
The first summarizes the results of an inventory of the educational activities of the adult population over a one-year period, and describes the
premises on which this inventory was based. In the middle section, the
paper examines what the people are like who engage in these activities,
how and why they come to enroll in them, and what if anything, they feel
they benefit from them. In the final section, the paper turns to the general question of potential audiences for programs of adult learning, and
then concludes with a forecast as to what an inventory of adult education
participation would be likely to yield if it were conducted about two decades from now.

In view of these goals, the main burden in this paper is with the
presentation and clarification of empirical evidence pertaining to adult
learning habits. The more difficult task of interpreting what this evidence means for the field of adult education is one which has been assigned, formally, to the discussants of this paper, and less formally to
you the participants at this conference.

I

During the summer of 1961 the National Opinion Research Center at
the University of Chicago was invited by the Carnegie Corporation of
New York to develop a research proposal to study the manpower investment of the American adult population in educational pursuits. Although
a rapidly expanding entity on the educational scene, the field of adult education had been faced for some time with an acute need for comprehen-

[*]This paper is based on research activities made possible by funds
granted by the Carnegie Corporation of New York. The statements made
and views expressed are solely the responsibility of the author.

sive information on the educational habits and practices of adults. Except for one study conducted in 1957 under the auspices of the Department of Health, Education and Welfare[1] and a Gallup poll conducted during the 40's,[2] the behavior in question had never before been examined on a national scale in this country. The central mandate of the inquiry, then, was to try to remedy this informational need by providing a comprehensive overview of the numbers and characteristics of adults engaged in studies of various subject matter through various methods of study and within various institutional contexts.

In initiating this inquiry the very first issue which had to be settled concerned the ranges of activity which were to be considered educational. Our problem, in short, was to decide what to include in and exclude from a national inventory of educational activities.

This question soon proved one for which there was no clear-cut nor widely accepted answer, but it was quite apparent that the scope of the investigation was going to vary radically depending on just how this question came to be resolved. The main problem was to avoid either a too narrow or a too broad conceptualization of an educational activity. At the one extreme it was tempting to equate educational activities with pursuits carried on in formal institutions of learning, but it was also obvious that this type of formal restriction was exactly what we did not want since it would exclude some of the most typical situations in which adults do encounter systematic learning experiences—situations such as on-the-job training or lessons with private instructors. Indeed, the whole institutional approach to the development of a definition was simply out of keeping with the spirit of a behavioral inventory of adult learning.

At the other extreme, of course, it was possible to formulate a definition strictly on the basis of the formal characteristics of an activity itself, or in terms of the consequences of an activity for the individual. While this strategy had more intrinsic appeal, the overwhelming problem here was that there would be virtually no way to exclude from consideration a host of activities where the consequences would certainly be edu-

---

1. U.S. Department of Health, Education and Welfare, "Participation in Adult Education," Circular No. 539 (Washington: U.S. Government Printing Office, 1959).

2. Reported in Adult Education Journal, IV, No. 2, April, 1945, 58.

cational—such as a visit to an aquarium—yet which clearly would fall beyond the range of any reasonable or workable definition of adult education.

The approach which was finally adopted, however, was closer to the behavioral than the institutional formulation. It was based on two considerations; the basic purpose of an activity and the nature of its organization. The first criterion was that the inventory would be confined to activities where the main purpose was to learn or acquire some type of knowledge, information, or skill. Activities with central functions more closely akin to recreation, fellowship, or remuneration were not to be included in the inventory even though the acquisition of knowledge, information, or skill might have been important by-products of them.

This criterion, then, allowed us to focus on the rationale of the activity itself rather than on the motives of the people who engaged in it. Thus "Bible classes" or "Sunday school classes" would be defined as educational since their main function is to teach about a religion, while "going to church" would not be included on the grounds that its main purpose would be worship. Similarly, "golf lessons" would be educational whereas "playing golf" would not.

The second criterion was that the activity had to be organized around some form of instruction. No restrictions were made as to the form the instruction could take, however. Regardless of whether it was received through classes, lecture series, discussion groups, private lessons, workshops, seminars, conferences, correspondence lessons, educational television programs, or on-the-job training, an activity was to be counted in the inventory as long as its central purpose was to impart some sort of knowledge, information, or skill.

Finally, we felt it was important not to exclude certain types of self-instruction from the study—especially in light of recent innovations in teaching machines and other home-study techniques. Accordingly, independent self-instruction was also to be covered in all situations where an individual consciously and systematically organized a program of study for himself and followed it for a period of not less than one month. Thus, persons teaching themselves a foreign language by means of tapes or long play recordings, or a musical instrument through home-study courses, were also to be counted in the inventory. General reading and other forms of casual information intake were by the same token ex-

91

cluded—except in cases where a person might claim that the reading was part of an organized program of study on some subject.

The distinction between courses involving instruction and self-taught educational pursuits rested on whether an activity involved any type of relationship between a student and teacher. In general, wherever some form of teacher-student relationship existed in the learning context— even if it was only of a rudimentary sort as in the case of correspondence lessons—the activity was classified as involving instruction. There are a number of borderline situations here, of course; the two most ambiguous are probably educational television courses and instruction by means of long-play recordings, tapes, or similar devices. It was between these two classes of activities, in fact, that the threshold between the presence and absence of an instructional relationship was considered to lie. In the case of educational television we reasoned that even though in most cases the direction of communication would be one-way only, at least the possibility would usually exist for a student to make some sort of contact with his instructor if he so desired. On television, instructors are typically identified by name and whereabouts. In the case of instruction by recordings, on the other hand, the possibility of two-way communication between student and teacher is much more remote. This issue may touch on the trivial, but these are the types of details which should be clarified before actual results are discussed.

It is clear that we dealt with a wide range of educational behavior in this study. In fact, our particular definition of the field of adult education is probably much wider than most uses of that term would suggest. Our inventory certainly covered many more learning situations than were included in the Office of Education's survey in 1957. In that study only activities experienced within the context of 'adult education classes or group meetings' were enumerated, and coverage of all correspondence studies, on-the-job training, private instruction, television courses, and other home-study activities was consequently omitted.

Once we had decided on what the inventory was to include, the next step was to translate these concerns into an appropriate study design. The basic plan of the inventory was to screen a sample of American households and have some responsible adult member of each household provide information on the educational activities of all members of that household during the previous 12 months. Since detailed information was needed about a large number of activities for which we were fairly certain there were not too many students, it was immediately clear that the inventory was going to require an extremely large sample of adults. Eventually, an area probability sample of over 13,000 households was decided on, and screening interviews were subsequently completed in 90 per cent of these households. This netted us basic information on the educational activities of 23,950 different adults. All of the estimates concerning adult education participation during 1961-62 derive from this source.

In a second stage of field work, additional information was collected by means of personal interviews with individuals randomly selected from the households originally screened. Altogether 2,845 interviews of approximately one hour's length were completed; any results which refer to educational experiences earlier than the previous year were derived from these interviews.[3]

Three types of educational statuses were identified in the inventory; those of full-time student, adult education participant, and participant in independent self-education.

A full-time student was defined as anyone who carried a full load of courses in some type of school or college, or anyone who reported more than three credit courses leading to some type of degree, diploma, or certificate in a high school or college.

The category of adult education participant, the status of most important concern to us in this study, was reserved for persons who had received instruction on a part-time basis. The category included persons studying both for credit and not-for-credit, and it covered all types of subject matter.

Finally, the third category consisted of persons who had been active in independent self-instruction for a period of at least one month during the previous year.

When the results of the household screening interviews were tabu-

---

3. The reader should also note that because recent participants were overselected in the sampling plan, a weighting system must be employed to restore representativeness. For tables based on the personal interviews, the 2,845 actual respondents become a weighted case base of 9,964.

lated, an extremely large amount of educational behavior was identified —in fact, considerably more than had been initially anticipated. It was estimated that nearly 25,000,000 adults—better than one in five—had been active in one or another form of educational pursuit over the period of the previous year (Table 1). Fifteen per cent of all adults, a total of over 17,000,000 persons, had been adult education participants and close to

TABLE 1

INVOLVEMENT OF ADULTS IN ORGANIZED EDUCATIONAL PURSUITS OVER A ONE-YEAR PERIOD
(June 1961 - May 1962)

	Per Cent of Sample Active in This Category (N=23,950)	Estimated Number of Persons[*]
(1) Full-time students	2.3	2,650,000
(2) Adult education participants	15.0	17,160,000
(3) Independent study participants	7.9	8,960,000
(4) Number of different adults active in any of these categories	21.8	24,810,000
(5) Number of different adults active other than as full-time students	20.2	23,020,000

[*] Based on an estimated total adult population of 114,000,000 persons as of June 1, 1962.

9,000,000 had tried to learn something new on their own. In addition, approximately two-and-a-half million adults had been full-time students according to the definition adopted in this study. All of these estimates, of course, covered just the adult population of the country—that is, persons either 21 or older, or married, or the head of a household.

Although these figures are obviously large, it is not possible to say very much about them in any comparative way, for there are no precisely comparable data either for earlier periods of American history or for other societies in contemporary times. The numbers are roughly equivalent to the total number of paid attendances at major league baseball games during a season,[4] represent about one-third the number of per-

4. The total paid attendances at major league baseball games dur-

94

sons who voted in the 1960 Presidential election,[5] and constitute considerably more Americans than have their teeth cleaned by a dentist over the period of a year.[6] Moreover, the number of different adults active in some type of educational pursuit in a one-year period is over half as large as the total number of persons under 20 who are enrolled in school in a year.[7]

Nonetheless, because of the lack of comparative data, about the only conclusion we can draw from these figures is that organized learning pursuits among the adult population of this country are by no means rare phenomena today. The numbers are certainly substantial and would merit attention in any complete study of American education.

If this many adults are active in educational pursuits over the period of just one year, then how many must engage in them over longer periods of time? To answer this question it is necessary to ask people about events which may have taken place many years earlier in their lives, and there are quite serious questions as to the accuracy of information of this type. About the best we can expect to obtain, then, is some approximation of the incidence of cumulative experiences with adult education.

In any event, when the respondents were asked if they had taken any educational courses since leaving school, as many as 47 per cent recalled being involved at least once. In addition, 38 per cent remembered having tried to teach themselves something on their own in the past, and all together a total of 61 per cent said they had engaged in one or another of those forms of learning experience at some time in the past.

When the reports on adult education courses were examined more

---

ing 1960, including the World Series games, was 20,261,000. U.S. Department of Commerce, Statistical Abstract of the United States, 1962 (Washington: U.S. Government Printing Office, 1962), p. 206.

5. Some 68,836,000 votes were cast for Presidential nominees in the 1960 election. Ibid., p. 361.

6. Between July, 1957, and June, 1958, adult Americans made a total of 17.7 million visits to dentists during which a teeth cleaning was performed. U.S. Department of Health, Education and Welfare, "Health Statistics" (Washington: U.S. Government Printing Office, November, 1958), p. 34.

7. A total of 44,118,000 persons between the ages of five and 20 were enrolled in school in 1960. U.S. Department of Commerce, Statistical Abstract of the United States, 1961 (Washington: U.S. Government Printing Office, 1961), p. 105.

thoroughly, it was found that most of the 47 per cent who had taken a course had done so just once or twice. About one adult in six (17 per cent), however, had received instruction on at least three separate occasions, and about one in a hundred reported being active nine or more times. Some quite interesting variations were found in the patterns of course taking revealed by the small group of extremely active individuals. The first and most common type was the individual who engaged in part-time education as an adult in order to complete a college degree. This type of pattern is exemplified in the following profile:

> Mr. X was a 31-year old suburban New York school teacher who had never stopped or even interrupted his own formal schooling. Ever since leaving school as a full-time student some five years previously, he had been enrolled in courses which would eventually lead him to a Ph.D. in modern languages. In the previous year he had taken three different courses in French literature, and at the time of the interview had worked off some 84 credit hours towards his Ph.D. He had never been enrolled in a non-credit adult education course. (Case #6031)

This pattern of learning activity can be easily distinguished from a second type where enrollments are confined to studies having no relation to any formal degree requirements. For example:

> Mrs. Y was a 41-year-old Seattle resident, a college graduate, wife and mother, who had been a school teacher prior to the birth of her first child. Her first adult education instruction was a course in sewing which she took at age 26. At 28 she took a mathematics course for credit—presumably a credit which she could apply towards a promotion on her job. At the age of 30 she took a course in Infant and Child Care, and also began a series of courses in International Affairs which she continued with off and on until she was 35. At 34 she took another credit course—this time in History, and at 35 a course in Public Speaking. For the next four years she was not active in courses at all, but she became active again at 39 when she attended a series of National Geographic lectures in Washington, D.C. During the previous year she had enrolled in a course titled 'Christian Education.' (Case #0029)

In this pattern of study the courses for the most part were non-credit, and none was connected with the requirements for any academic degree. Mrs. Y's studies, rather, were related to a much wider variety of life roles, to those of homemaker, parent, member of the community, and member of the labor force. Her experiences also differ in that they are characterized by periodic rather than uninterrupted involvement.

A third pattern among the highly active was that which combined each of these other two patterns—that is, where the first experiences were in degree-connected studies, and where later studies branched into new and quite unrelated spheres of subject matter. One respondent who illustrated this pattern was the following:

> Mr. Z was a 39-year-old Palo Alto electronics engineer who between his mid-20's and mid-30's spent a total of 11 years as a part-time credit student, and eventually obtained both a Bachelor's and Master's degree in Engineering. After completing the Master's degree, he began to enroll in courses outside of the degree program. At 36 he took a course in analog computers and another in digital computer mathematics; at 37 courses in electronic timing circuits and statistics; at 38 courses in literature, Zen Buddhism, Psychology, Digital Computer Programming and Management Development. Most recently, at 39, he had joined a Great Books group. (Case #0476)

In this particular case history, the habit of continuous study became established through formal degree studies, and when the degree requirements were completed, a well entrenched study habit was extended into completely new realms of learning. This particular respondent had been continuously engaged in educational courses for a period of 15 years.

These three examples represent interesting profiles, but they are rather atypical cases since the much more common mode of experience was for a participant to have been active just once or twice.

An analysis of the subjects adults had studied during the previous year indicated that the content of adult education is in the main quite different from that which one encounters during regular school days. Not only were adult education studies primarily non-credit (only 26 per cent of all courses which involved instruction were taken for credit towards some kind of degree, diploma, or certificate) but the subject matter itself was overwhelmingly non-academic. The subjects recorded in the inventory were concentrated quite heavily within the vocational and recreational fields, and subjects a part of a more traditional academic schooling all together made up just an eighth of the total courses studied (Table 2).

All together, about one-third of adult learning pursuits during the previous year were in the vocational sphere while one-fifth were in the recreational (34 and 19 per cent respectively). The fields of academic education, religion, and home and family life subjects each claimed one-eighth of the total studies, while all other categories had a relatively minor place in the over-all distribution of studies.[8] In this regard, it was revealing

---

8. The personal development category was built in order to cluster together a wide variety of miscellaneous types of subjects all aimed at

TABLE 2

TYPES OF SUBJECT MATTER STUDIED IN ADULT EDUCATION
COURSES AND IN INDEPENDENT SELF-STUDY
(June 1961 - May 1962)

Category of Subject	Adult Education Courses (Per Cent)	Independent Self-Study (Per Cent)	Total (Per Cent)
Vocational	37	26	34
Hobbies and Recreations	16	25	19
Home and Family Life	7	21	12
Academic Subjects	11	15	12
Religious	15	5	12
Personal Development	6	5	5
Public Affairs and Current Events	4	2	3
Miscellaneous	3	1	3
Total	99	100	100
Base	4649	2221	6870
No information	19	5	24
Total courses	4668	2226	6894

that as few as three per cent of the total courses were in the public affairs or current events sphere. On the basis of popular stereotypes about
adult education, one might have expected a considerably stronger representation from this field of studies. However, if there is any single image
of adult education which is inappropriate, it is that which equates the
field with Great Books courses or current events study groups. In combination, the persons involved in these studies made up less than two per
cent of the total participants.

It was quite clear from these results that the major emphasis in

---

helping people expand themselves in the areas of physical fitness, health,
personality development, interpersonal and social skills, or basic reading, writing, and language facility. The category is therefore organized
in terms of the functions or consequences of studies, and not at all on the
basis of any substantive connection between the subjects. It is the general notion of physical, psychological, or social adjustment which provides the organizing rationale for linking together these otherwise quite
unconnected subjects.

adult learning is on the practical rather than the academic; on the applied rather than the theoretical; and on skills rather than knowledge or values. Subject matter directly useful to the performance of everyday tasks and obligations, for example, represented a significant segment of the total activities. Taken together the vocational and home and family life categories alone represented 44 per cent of all adult education courses studied and 47 per cent of all subjects people studied on their own. On the other hand, the academic, religious, and public affairs categories—the areas which one might consider more representative of the realms of ideas and values—made up just 30 per cent of the courses taken and 22 per cent of the independent studies. These comparisons illustrate the predominantly pragmatic quality of adult education in America.

The study also revealed that the types of subjects people study on their own are quite different from those in which they receive instruction (Table 2). The content of independent studies, for example, was about evenly divided between four segments—vocational, recreational, home and family life, and all other categories. Educational pursuits which involved instruction, on the other hand, were heavily dominated with vocational subject matter and no other category came even close to the job-related.

There was evidence, too, that some of these independent learning pursuits may have been of quite recent development. A number of the specific course titles people frequently studied on their own were in areas strongly influenced either by recent innovations in teaching machines, changes in patterns of leisure time use, or efforts by commercial interests to enter the educational field. For example, 61 per cent of all courses in foreign languages were studied without the benefit of formal instruction, and this undoubtedly reflects at least in part the influence of recent campaigns by newspapers to promote subscriptions through offers of low-cost foreign language instruction via long-play recordings. In addition, just under half of the persons who took courses in speed reading did so through methods of self-instruction, and this too reflects recent innovations in home-study techniques. Moreover, since half of all courses in music were self-taught, one might guess that a substantial number of Americans no longer laugh when their friends sit down at the piano. Of course, it may be they are now laughing even harder, for it is quite impossible for us to evaluate the quality of the learning experiences people get from self-study

99

methods. In terms of the quantity of activity, however, the results were impressive. And in view of the prospects for even further developments of this type, one might anticipate that independent self-instruction will become an even more prominent feature of American adult education in the near future.

Thus, just as the content of adult learning differs markedly from that of an academic curriculum, so too do adult learning methods deviate from the more conventional forms. Even if we leave aside independent self-education entirely, almost half of all adult education courses were encountered outside of traditional classroom settings (Table 3). Although no other single method was very extensively employed, the combined use of the group discussion, the public lecture, correspondence study, private instruction and on-the-job training accounted for approximately 45

TABLE 3

METHODS OF STUDY EMPLOYED IN ADULT EDUCATION
COURSES WHICH INVOLVED INSTRUCTION

Method of Study	Per Cent of Total Courses Studied by This Method	Estimated Number of Different Persons Who Studied by This Method
Attended classes	56	10,450,000
Attended group discussions	11	2,300,000
Attended lectures or talks	10	2,220,000
Correspondence study	8	1,750,000
Private teachers	8	1,670,000
On-the-job training	8	1,680,000
Educational television	2	290,000
All other methods	.. †	... ‡
Total	103*	17,160,000*
Base	4497	
Information not given	173	
Total courses	4670	

*Does not total to 100 per cent (or to the sum of the figures in the column) because some courses were studied by more than one method.

†Less than one per cent.

‡Too few to estimate.

100

per cent of all courses in which instruction was received at all.

One of the most surprising results in this regard was that television had apparently failed to make much of an impact as a medium of formal adult instruction. Only one-and-a-half per cent of all courses studied during the previous year had been taken via television instruction and only 290,000 persons were estimated to have followed an educational course on television during this time. From some points of view, of course, this estimate would represent a sizeable number of adult students, but it by no means came close to the one-and-three-quarter million adults estimated to have taken a correspondence course over the same period of time. Indeed, of the major home-study forms, television study is still very much overshadowed by correspondence study.

This result is all the more puzzling since in discussions of television audiences one usually deals with audience figures at least ten times this large, and sometimes several hundred times this large.[9] The puzzle, then, is why a medium capable of attracting the largest audiences of all times should attract so few followers in its formal educational efforts. Since the sample was designed to give proportionate representation to persons living in all types of geographical situations in this country, it would also give proportionate representation to persons living within the exposure ranges of an ETV station, and indeed, we had actually interviewed in at least 20 urban locations where an educational television station was in operation at the time the inventory was conducted. The explanation for the low estimates, in other words, could not be due to the fact that the sample did not give fair representation to householders able to receive signals from ETV stations.

Although open-circuit instructional television is still very much in a developmental stage in this country, there may be reason to believe that factors other than sheer availability may be behind this result. In the conclusions of a recent study of the uses of television, for example, the 'average American viewer' was described as follows:

---

9. For example, it is estimated that some 70 million U.S. adults watched or listened to the first Kennedy-Nixon television debate in the 1960 presidential campaign. See Elihu Katz and Jacob J. Feldman, "The Kennedy-Nixon Debates: A Survey of Surveys," Studies in Public Communication, No. 4, 1962, p. 130.

He would like TV to be more informative and educational but certainly not at the expense of entertainment. Aside from the day's news and weather—which he watches regularly—he rarely uses the set as a deliberate source of information, and he is extremely unlikely to turn on serious and informative public affairs presentations, even if he is watching while they are on the air. . . . Television, among the home sources of mass communication, has its greatest comparative advantage in the field of entertainment. . . . It is television, by a wide margin, that is turned to for relaxation and diversion.[10]

It might be the case, then, that television has come to be almost exclusively identified by the American public as a medium of light entertainment, and if this is true, then it might also be the case that no matter how much instructional fare were made available on the medium, it would still be preferred for other purposes, and other sources or channels would still be seen as more appropriate for systematic learning.

With regard to the institutions from which adults received instruction, there was a marked contrast from the channels used in getting a formal education (Table 4). Although high schools, colleges, and universities unquestionably play an important role in adult education, the inventory nonetheless revealed that more adults study outside the formal school system than within it.

Altogether, only a third of the courses were studied within the regular school system. When courses taken in private schools and community adult education centers were added to those taken in high schools, colleges, or universities, still less than half of the total had been studied in institutions whose primary functions could be said to lie in the field of education. In fact in terms of over-all numbers, more adults had studied in churches or synagogues than in any other type of institution. This instruction was confined almost exclusively to religious training, of course, and 86 per cent of the courses taken in churches or synagogues were in religion. The activities of business and industry were also heavily concentrated within one specific subject area: 79 per cent of the courses were in vocational subjects. It is clear, then, that religious and economic institutions play highly specialized roles in the field of adult instruction.

The most important aspect of these findings is that an actual ma-

10. Gary A. Steiner, The People Look at Television (New York: Knopf, 1963), pp. 228-29.

TABLE 4

ESTIMATES OF COURSES ATTENDED AT DIFFERENT
SPONSORING INSTITUTIONS*

Sponsoring Institution	Per Cent of All Courses Which Involved Attendance at Classes, Lectures, or Group Discussions	Estimated Number of Different Persons Who Attended Classes, Lectures, or Group Discussions
Churches and Synagogues	21	3,260,000
Colleges and Universities	21	2,640,000
Community Organizations‡	15	2,240,000
Business and Industry§	12	1,860,000
Elementary and Secondary Schools	12	1,740,000
Private Schools	7	1,120,000
Government—all levels	7	1,050,000
Armed Forces	4	480,000
All other sponsors	2	240,000
Total	101	13,360,000[†]
Base	3305	
No information	83	
Total courses studied by classes, group discussions, or public lectures	3388	

[*] This table covers only those courses which involved attendance at classes, lectures, talks, or group discussions—in effect, only those activities in which people made direct contact with an institution in order to receive instruction.

[†] Does not total to number of persons listed in the column because some persons studied different courses at different sponsoring institutions.

[‡] Includes community centers, adult education centers, YMCA's, libraries, museums, and other related institutions.

[§] Excludes all on-the-job training.

jority of the learning activities pursued by adults were experienced within institutions whose main concerns lie in areas other than education. This would suggest that many of the adults who come to engage in formal learning activities may do so primarily in relation to the demands and expectations made on them by the organizations to which they establish connections and attachments.

II

In this section we will focus on the people who engage in adult education activities. To start, we will examine their background characteristics in relation to those of the total adult population and discuss how various of these factors affect rates of educational participation. Following this, we will then examine how people first come to enroll in adult education courses, what they expect to gain by taking courses, and what they feel they have gained after they have been enrolled.

To start, let us try to characterize the one adult in five who either took an adult education course or was engaged in independent self-study between June, 1961, and June, 1962.

After investigating a large number of personal, socio-economic, and ecological characteristics, three factors were found which persistently distinguished participants from non-participants: they differed in age, in the amount of formal education they had had, and in where they lived.

The first distinctive feature of the adult education participant is that he is younger than the 'average' American adult. The median age of participants was 36-1/2 years: this was better than six years younger than that found in the sample as a whole. Thus, over half of all participants were under 40 years of age, and nearly four in five were under the age of 50. In terms of <u>rates</u> of participation, moreover, there were vast differences between persons in different age brackets: the rates fell from a high of 29 per 100 among adults in their 20's to four per 100 among persons 70 or above (Table 5).

Other than for age, however, there were no other personal or life cy-

TABLE 5

RATES OF PARTICIPATION IN EDUCATIONAL
PURSUITS, BY AGE

	Under 20	20-29	30-39	40-49	50-59	60-69	70 and Over
Per cent who studied any subject by any method	16	29	25	21	16	10	4
Base =	(262)	(4,526)	(5,119)	(5,038)	(3,827)	(2,861)	(2,044)

cle characteristics which served to set the adult education participant apart from the general population. The participants were about equally divided between men and women, and there were only slight discrepancies in religious background between participants and the general population. A slight under-representation of Negroes among the participants completely disappeared when Negroes were compared with whites of similar educational background. And a slight over-representation of married persons and under-representation of widows and widowers could be explained in terms of the different ages of persons in these statuses. Besides age, the only life-cycle characteristic which made any difference at all in rates of participation was parenthood. Sixty per cent of the participants had at least one child under the age of 21, and this constituted a six-to-five over-representation of parents. We will discuss this finding later in this section.

The second outstanding feature of the adult education participant is that he is better educated than the average American adult. The participants had attended school 12.2 years on the average compared with 11.5 years for all adults in the sample, but the real extent of this difference is much more sharply expressed by comparing rates of participation. During the previous year, these rates ranged from 4 per cent among persons with no formal schooling at all to 47 per cent among those who had attended more than 16 years.

As a consequence of these basic differences in schooling, adult education participants were also more likely to hold white collar than blue collar jobs, and had a median family income almost $1,200 higher than that of the average American adult.

Among these three socio-economic measures, however, education was found to have by far the most powerful influence on rates of participation (Table 6). Although occupation and income did have independent effects, no combination of income and occupational conditions was found which could contribute an effect which superceded that of having more education. Taken together, of course, the influence of all three factors was extremely strong: a person who had been to college, who worked in a white collar occupation, and who made more than $7,000 a year was about six times more likely to have been active in adult education during the previous year than a person who had never been beyond grade school, who worked in a blue collar occupation and whose family income was

TABLE 6

RATES OF PARTICIPATION IN ADULT EDUCATION, BY EDUCATION, OCCUPATION, AND FAMILY INCOME
(Per cent who studied any subject by any method)

Occupation	Grade School			High School			College		
	Under $4,000	$4,000-6,999	$7,000 & Over	Under $4,000	$4,000-6,999	$7,000 & Over	Under $4,000	$4,000-6,999	$7,000 & Over
Blue collar	7 (1,463)	8 (964)	11 (389)	20 (1,207)	21 (1,937)	23 (1,126)	37 (136)	40 (269)	37 (229)
White collar	9 (125)	11 (176)	14 (122)	22 (371)	21 (1,081)	29 (1,340)	37 (190)	45 (704)	43 (1,698)

less than $4,000 a year.

Although a less prominent feature than either age or education, the participants could also be differentiated from the general population in terms of their geographical dispersion. First, residents of large metropolitan areas were over-represented among participants, while persons living in small cities, small towns, and rural areas were under-represented. Within the large urban areas, however, it was only those living in suburbs or outskirts who were over-represented; those living in the central cities were not. The surprising part of this finding, however, was that the different rates of study between residents of central cities and suburban areas was not simply a function of the higher socio-economic characteristics of the suburban dwellers. Indeed, the differences were found both among those who had completed high school and those who had not (Table 7). Among the better educated respondents, moreover, these central city-suburban differences were found to be localized within one particular area of subject-matter, namely recreational studies. High school graduates who lived in suburban areas were almost twice as likely to have studied some recreational topic as were their educational counterparts who lived inside the city limits, but on all other categories of subject, the differences were minimal. This channeling effect was not found among persons who had not completed high school, however, and although the over-all rates of study among these suburban dwellers were also higher, their additional studies were not directed toward any specific subject matter.

A second distinctive geographical characteristic of adult education participants was their representation by region. Although numerically more participants lived in the South than in any of the other three main regions of the country, it was only the residents of western states who were over-represented in the ranks of adult education participants. The regional imbalance was particularly strong on the West Coast, however. Persons living in the three Pacific states made up some 20 per cent of all adult education participants while representing only 14 per cent of the total population.

While the highest rates of participation were found in the West, the second highest were found in the South, and this was a quite surprising finding in view of the over-all educational attainment of the residents of different regions (Table 8). On practically any criterion the South would

107

TABLE 7

RATES OF PARTICIPATION IN ADULT EDUCATION, BY SIZE AND
TYPE OF COMMUNITY AND EDUCATION
(Per cent who studied any subject by any method)

Education	Large Cities		Middle Size Cities		Small Cities	Small Town and Rural
	Central City	Suburbs	Central City	Suburbs		
Persons who completed high school	28 (1,413)	34 (1,655)	29 (2,501)	35 (2,478)	30 (1,644)	22 (2,117)
Persons who did not complete high school	9 (1,210)	12 (967)	10 (2,440)	16 (1,761)	8 (1,731)	8 (3,275)

108

be found to be the region with the lowest over-all educational attainment, and by a considerable margin.[11] Yet the South also displayed the second highest rate of participation in adult education. The finding was rather perplexing.

TABLE 8

RATES OF PARTICIPATION IN EDUCATIONAL PURSUITS,
BY REGION AND EDUCATION
(Per cent who studied any subject by any method)

Education	Northeast	North Central	South	West
Persons who completed high school	26 (3,135)	27 (3,468)	30 (3,032)	37 (2,209)
Persons who did not complete high school	6 (2,472)	9 (3,252)	10 (4,174)	18 (1,555)

When this result was investigated further, it was found to be related solely to one category of subject matter, namely, religious studies. Among both high school graduates and non-graduates, rates of religious study were very much higher in the South than in either northern region, and they were even higher in the South than in the West. The difference in the over-all rates of study between the South and the North, then, was produced solely by the higher rates of religious study in the South.

In contrast, three areas of subject matter were found to have contributed to the higher over-all incidence of study in the West: the principal differences were found in the field vocational studies, but important secondary differences were also contributed by the academic and recreational categories.

The main regional differences, then, were that westerners had defi-

---

11. For example, in 1960 the median years of schooling completed by persons 25 years and over in different regions was 12.0 in the West, 10.7 in both the Northeast and North Central regions, and 9.1 in the South. U.S. Department of Commerce, Bureau of the Census, United States Census of Population, 1960: General Social and Economic Characteristics (Washington: United States Government Printing Office, 1962), Table 115, pp. 1-260.

nitely accelerated rates of study in the vocational, academic, and recreational spheres, while southerners were considerably more likely to study religion.

By way of summary of these materials, one might compose a sort of social profile of the typical adult education participant: he is just as often a woman as a man; is typically under 40; has completed high school or better; enjoys an above-average income; works full-time and most often in a white collar occupation; is typically white and Protestant; is married and a parent; lives in an urbanized area and more likely in suburbs than inside a large city; and is found in all parts of the country, but more frequently on the West Coast than would be expected by chance.

When rates of participation in adult education were examined among men and women of different ages, some quite interesting discrepancies emerged (Table 9). In general, of course, there was not much difference

TABLE 9

RATES OF PARTICIPATION IN EDUCATIONAL
ACTIVITIES, BY SEX AND AGE

Rate	Men			Women		
	Under 35	35-54	55 and Above	Under 35	35-54	55 and Above
Per cent who studied any subject by any method	33	21	9	25	21	10
Base =	(3,287)	(4,684)	(2,920)	(3,847)	(4,900)	(3,420)

at all in the rates of study among men and women: some 21 per cent of all men compared with 19 per cent of all women had been active during the previous year, and while this difference is statistically significant it certainly does not have much practical significance. In the subsequent analysis, however, it was found that men under 35 had rates of study which were substantially higher than those of women the same age (33 per cent compared with 25 per cent). Older men and women, on the other hand, revealed practically identical rates of involvement with adult education. This finding was an unexpected one, then, since it had been well

110

hidden in the over-all comparison of men and women.

The most obvious explanation for this result seemed somehow tied up with the differential effects of family life on young men and young women. Since the difference occurred during the phase of the life-cycle when family responsibilities are very heavy, it seemed likely that the difference was a simple reflection of the fact that family duties more seriously curtail the away-from-home activities of young mothers than of young fathers. To explore this possibility, we compared the rates of study of young adults who both had and did not have children, and when this was done we found that it was indeed the impact of parenthood which had produced the differential rates of study (Table 10). There were no differences at all in the activity rates of young men and women who did not have children (29 per cent each) but very substantial differences were found between the participation rates of young fathers and young mothers (34 per cent and 23 per cent, respectively). In fact, the impact of parenthood appeared to have quite opposite effects on the educational behavior of husbands and wives; the rates of study for mothers were lower than for non-mothers, but among men they were higher among fathers than non-fathers. In seeking out evidence to explain one result, then, we had uncovered another finding for which further explanation seemed necessary.

The most likely interpretation of this second result seemed connected in some way to economic considerations: since men who have children also have additional financial burdens, we reasoned, then they might take courses more frequently in order to learn subjects and skills which will help them to supplement their incomes. If so, then their heightened rates of study should be pretty much confined to the sphere of vocational studies. On the other hand, it might also be the case that since parenthood probably commits a man more firmly to a home-and-family role, the accelerated rates of study might be produced primarily by increased participation in courses pertaining to home and family life subjects and skills. Or indeed, perhaps the explanation was that enrollment in educational courses constitutes a socially acceptable way for a man to gain respite from the confusion in his home. The result did confirm, in any event, that at least as far as men were concerned adult education activities did not attract primarily the lonely or the isolated: if anything on this score, the results indicated quite the opposite.

111

TABLE 10

LIFE CYCLE POSITION AND PARTICIPATION IN ADULT EDUCATION

Rate	Number of Children under 21											
	Age under 35				Age 35-54				Age 55 and Above			
	Men		Women		Men		Women		Men		Women	
	One or More	None	One or More	None	One or More	None	One or More	None	One or More	None	One or More	None
Per cent who studied any subject by any method	34	29	23	29	24	16	22	18	14	8	8	10
Base =	(2,036)	(1,349)	(2,893)	(993)	(3,072)	(1,714)	(2,877)	(2,098)	(333)	(2,727)	(131)	(3,421)

When rates of study in specific types of subject matter were examined for both fathers and non-fathers, the issue was considerably cleared up, and the difference was pinned down to the sphere of vocational learning. Our original economic explanation, then, seemed the one most probably correct. With regard to home and family life studies, only small differences were found between parents and non-parents, and this suggested, somewhat surprisingly, that one's role as a parent had little direct impact on this particular sphere of adult learning. The data did reveal a relationship between parental status and religious studies, however: although this evidence was far from clearcut, rates of religious study were slightly higher among parents than among non-parents.

While these results are hardly startling, they do demonstrate that life-cycle position represents an important determinant of the extent to which adults will participate in organized learning pursuits. What are the kinds of life situations, then, which lead people to enroll in courses in the first place? When the participants in our study were asked about this, they provided us with some quite useful information. First, however, we learned that initial contacts with adult education courses typically occur quite early during adult life. Two out of every three adults who had ever taken a course did so before their thirtieth birthday. Seven of eight did so before they were 40. Moreover, there were some revealing differences in the recruitment ages of men and women: men were more likely than women to have taken their first course while in their twenties, but proportionately more women were recruited both before the age of 20 and after the age of 40.[12] This probably reflects two tendencies. First, since more girls than boys drop out of school before the age of twenty,[13] the pool of teen-agers from which adult education recruits could be drawn would be disproportionately female. But second, since women who have families are likely to suffer rather severe restrictions on their freedom of movement during the twenties and thirties,

---

12. The proportions of men who took their first adult education course during their teens, 20's, 30's, and 40's or older were, respectively, 17, 52, 19, and 11. The comparable figures for women were 22, 43, 18, and 18.

13. For example, among 18 and 19 year-olds in the U.S. population of 1960, the proportions no longer in school were 70 per cent of girls and 52 per cent of boys. U.S. Department of Commerce (1961), op. cit., p. 105.

their proportionately higher recruitment after the age of forty probably reflects enrollment which might have taken place earlier had family considerations not interfered.

The first experiences adults have with continuing education are typically job-related ones (Table 11). This is particularly true for men; about four out of five of the men in our sample of participants took their first courses either in vocational or academic subjects—fields, that is,

TABLE 11

SUBJECT MATTER STUDIED IN FIRST ADULT EDUCATION
COURSES, BY SEX

Type of Subject	Men (per cent)	Women (per cent)	All Participants (per cent)
Vocational	65	46	55
Academic	15	10	13
Hobbies and recreations	6	16	11
Home and family life	1	14	8
Personal development	3	5	4
Religion	2	6	4
Public affairs	2	2	2
Miscellaneous	5	2	4
Total	99	101	101
Base	2296	2296	4592
No information	0	11	11
Total (weighted)	2296	2307	4603

which would have a direct bearing on their occupational placement. Of the first courses taken by women, the largest category was also the vocational one, but these constituted less than half of their first courses (46 per cent). In comparison with men, rather sizeable numbers of women first enrolled to study home and family life subject matter (14 per cent) or subjects connected directly with leisure time interests (16 per cent).

When the respondents were asked how they first came to enroll in an adult education course, four main types of answer were given. First, about one person in three mentioned preparation for a new job—either a first job after leaving school, a new job replacing one already held, or vocational training encountered either upon entry into or discharge from the Armed Services.

A second group made up of about 20 per cent of all participants mentioned additional training in relation to the job they already held. Half of these indicated that the training was either a condition of their employment or had been suggested by their employer.

All together, then, a majority of the participants recalled that it was some sort of occupational contingency which first led them into further studies in adult life.

A third group consisting of approximately 30 per cent of the participants answered in terms of some type of interpersonal influence they had experienced—influences either from employers, family members, friends, or even other less intimate sources. (One women had been talked into taking piano lessons by a salesman.) The fact that three participants in 10 spontaneously associated other people with their recruitment to adult education certainly suggests that interpersonal influence may play a quite significant role in bringing potential adult education participants into actual enrollment.

One remaining cluster of persons consisting of about one participant in 10 mentioned some type of change in their family status in relation to their initial ventures with continuing education. These family influences were about evenly divided between situations of family expansion and situations in which one's responsibilities had become lessened—in particular, when children had grown up.

These, then, were the main things people remembered about how they first came to enroll in courses: job preparation and job advancement contexts, personal relationships, and changes in family status or composition.

As could be anticipated, of course, the situations identified by men and women in this regard were not at all the same. Many more men than women talked about job-related contexts, and all together two-thirds of men associated some vocational situation with their original enrollment. Job preparation situations were recalled over job advancement ones by a ratio of about two-to-one. In addition, it turned out that at least one male student in six had encountered his first experiences with adult education while in the Armed Forces. On the other hand, practically all of the participants who first turned to adult education in relation to some type of family contingency were women.

One finding which was more of a surprise was that women were much more likely than men to mention the influence of family or friends in relation to their original enrollment. More men than women, however, mentioned influences stemming from social contacts other than with one's family or friends. Thus, although a substantial number of participants referred to the influence of other people, women were more likely to mention influences stemming from their primary social relationships, and men contacts with persons in secondary social settings.

More direct evidence on the uses of adult education by persons in different phases of the life cycle emerged from an analysis of the reasons people gave to explain why they had enrolled in the courses they had taken most recently [14] (Table 12). The most pronounced findings in this regard were the more obvious ones, of course, namely that vocational considerations are of more relevance to men than to women, and that people less frequently turn to adult education for purposes of job preparation as they grow older. However, the downward trend in the endorsement of this goal was arrested after the age of 50 among men. This would suggest that some men turn to adult education to learn new vocational skills after they retire, or perhaps are displaced from obsolescent jobs. In any event, during the 30's the main vocational reason men had for taking adult education courses shifted from job preparation to job advancement. This switch in vocational emphasis did not occur until the 40's among women.

In the main it is job-centered reasons which most frequently propel younger adults into adult education participation, and by comparison the uses made of adult education by older adults are much less pragmatic and utilitarian. For example, the proportion of participants who endorsed the goal "to become a better informed person" was considerably higher

---

14. The approach which was taken to appraise the reasons why people took courses was as follows: first, a number of widely held notions as to why people take courses were formulated into phrases about how courses might be helpful to a person, and participants were asked whether any of these had been relevant to them at the time of their most recent enrollment. Following this, they were asked if there were any other ways they had hoped the course would be helpful to them.

TABLE 12

REASONS FOR TAKING MOST RECENT ADULT EDUCATION COURSE, BY SEX, AND AGE AT TIME OF ENROLLMENT

Reasons	Men				Women			
	Under 30	30-39	40-49	50 and Over	Under 30	30-39	40-49	50 and Over
Prepare for new job	48%	39%	29%	33%	41%	27%	24%	17%
Help on incumbent job	40	50	48	37	19	20	25	18
Become better informed	35	40	27	57	31	41	41	47
Spare time enjoyment	10	16	19	28	24	30	24	29
Home-centered tasks	7	15	6	2	13	24	21	16
Other everyday tasks	10	16	7	3	9	9	8	22
Meet new people	11	16	12	19	23	20	15	22
Escape the daily routine	6	8	4	8	13	16	15	16
None of these, or don't know	7	4	6	6	4	5	9	4
Total	174*	204*	158*	193*	177*	192*	182*	191*
Base	1010	578	320	144	842	548	420	223
No information	98	70	34	28	125	24	36	58
Total (weighted)	1108	648	354	172	967	572	456	281

*Does not total to 100 per cent because some persons gave more than one reason.

among adults over the age of 50. Although this statement could certainly be considered a meaningful rationale for studies of practically anything, it would seem to be more directly applicable to persons concerned with the acquisition of knowledge and information rather than skills, and also a goal which would be endorsed more often by persons who do not have any well articulated utilitarian purpose in mind at the time they enroll in a course. In other words, endorsement of this statement would probably reflect at least a modicum of intrinsic intellectual commitment to the subject matter in question.

This general shift away from a pragmatic orientation to adult education was also reflected in the extent to which leisure-centered goals were endorsed by men in different age-groups. Among men, the emphasis on learning for spare time enjoyment was more prominent in each successively older age-group. The statement "spend my spare time more enjoyably," in fact, was selected as an enrollment motive almost three times more often by men over 50 than by men under 30 (28 per cent compared with 10 per cent). A similar shift was not found among women, but a substantial number of the younger women were already using adult education in relation to leisure time interests.

More generally, of course, these results probably reflect only the fact that the learning interests of younger men are heavily dominated with concerns about making a living, while those of older men are not.

One quite interesting finding was that women were more likely than men to use adult education not only in relation to home and family life goals, but also for purposes of meeting new people, and in order to get away from daily routines. With respect to establishing social contacts, the gap was particularly strong among participants under 30: among these persons, the statement "meet new and interesting people" was selected by 23 per cent of women and only 11 per cent of men.

The widest gap in the endorsement of the goal "to get away from the daily routine," on the other hand, was found among persons in their 40's. Among participants of this age, it was relevant to 15 per cent of the women and only 4 per cent of the men. These findings would suggest, in any event, that not insignificant numbers of women use adult education both for purposes of cultivating new social relationships and in order to escape from the repetitiveness of everyday experiences.

Quite revealing findings were also obtained regarding the ways in which adult education is used by persons at different levels of the social class hierarchy. Earlier, we noted that the socio-economic indicators (income, occupation, and in particular, years of formal schooling) all were positively related with rates of participation in educational pursuits over a one-year period. In addition, however, socio-economic level was also found to be quite strongly related to the goals people have in mind when they do enroll in these studies (Table 13).

TABLE 13

REASONS FOR TAKING COURSES STUDIED DURING PREVIOUS FIVE YEARS, BY SEX AND SOCIO-ECONOMIC STATUS

Reasons	Socio-economic Status					
	Men			Women		
	Low	Medi-um	High	Low	Medi-um	High
Prepare for new job	59%	39%	34%	41%	29%	20%
Help on incumbent job	44	43	50	13	18	24
Become better informed	25	38	45	39	39	40
Spare time enjoyment	6	12	18	16	32	31
Home-centered tasks	2	8	8	26	21	13
Other everyday tasks	8	12	8	18	12	7
Meet new people	9	11	13	23	16	21
Escape the daily routine	-	7	7	16	20	15
None of these, or don't know	4	8	3	7	2	7
Total	157*	178*	186*	199*	189*	178*
Base	212	375	650	207	427	628
No information	23	31	70	41	46	56
Total (weighted)	235	406	720	248	473	684

*Does not total to 100 per cent because some persons gave more than one reason.

First, a direct relationship was found between socio-economic levels and the types of vocational reasons which were stressed. Men and women of lower socio-economic status, for example, were much more likely to use adult education for purposes of job preparation than for occupational advancement, while the opposite was true for participants from higher

119

SES levels. In lower social class positions, in other words, it would appear that the main function of vocational education is to place people into new jobs; at higher levels, on the other hand, vocational education functions much more to advance one's position on a job already held.

A second important difference was that among both men and women learning in relation to spare time enjoyment received much stronger emphasis in the higher socio-economic levels. In fact, there were virtually no men in the lower third of the socio-economic continuum who had enrolled in their most recent course for purposes of leisure time enjoyment. Across the middle and upper thirds of this distribution, however, the endorsement of spare-time goals trebled: it moved from 6 to 12 to 18 per cent. Among women these reasons were also endorsed more frequently in the upper SES levels (from 16 to 21 to 31 per cent in the low, middle, and upper thirds, respectively). Moreover, for women of middle or higher socio-economic status, leisure time considerations were motives for enrollment more frequently than either job preparation, job advancement, or homemaking concerns.

In addition, among women the use of adult education to learn homemaking subjects and skills was negatively related to socio-economic level. The proportion of women who enrolled in courses in order to learn how to carry out tasks and duties around the home dropped from 26 to 21 to 13 per cent across the three SES levels identified.

There are very pronounced ways in which the uses of adult education differ across the social class spectrum: at lower SES levels adult education is used primarily to learn the skills necessary for coping with the necessities of everyday living. Among men, learning concerns were almost exclusively vocational, and particularly strong emphasis was placed on finding jobs. Among women of lower socio-economic status, adult education uses were heavily concentrated in both the vocational and homemaking areas.

As one moves up the social class ladder vocational concerns not only become less prevalent but they shift from concerns about finding employment to concerns about getting ahead in a line of work already entered. In general, however, there is an over-all shift away from learning for purposes of basic life adjustment, and an accompanying increment of concern with less pressing contingencies such as the enrichment of one's spare time.

How much do people benefit from the courses they take? Do they find these experiences at all useful? In general, our results indicated that they do. When asked how much they had gained from the courses they had taken most recently, 63 per cent said they benefited "a great deal"; 23 per cent said "some"; and only 13 per cent said "not very much."

A more stringent criterion by which to evaluate the effectiveness of adult studies, of course, is to determine whether the courses are helpful in the ways that people want them to be. In other words, while a person might say a course had helped him in a number of ways, the crucial question should be whether or not it satisfied the goals which led him to enroll in the first place. To evaluate course-taking on this criterion, "effectiveness indices" were worked out for each of the different reasons people gave for taking courses: these consisted simply of the proportion who said their most recent course had definitely been helpful to them in the ways they had hoped it would be (Table 14).

When these results were examined they suggested that adult education courses may be a lot more effective in satisfying some goals than in satisfying others. The two most important findings were (a) that

TABLE 14

EFFECTIVENESS OF ADULT STUDIES

Ways in Which Course Was Helpful	Index of Effectiveness*	Base[†]
Help on incumbent job	.90	(1,330)
Learned home centered skills	.87	(554)
To become better informed	.86	(1,528)
Met new people	.80	(635)
Learned to spend spare time more enjoyably	.77	(837)
Escaped from daily routine	.73	(434)
Learned other everyday skills	.72	(435)
Helped prepare for a new job	.57	(1,492)

*Proportion for whom course was helpful in that way among those who wanted it to be helpful in that way.

[†]Number of persons who wanted course to be helpful in this way (weighted).

121

adult education courses were most effective when people enrolled in order to learn more about their jobs; and (b) that they were least effective in preparing people to enter a new job or occupation. The discrepancy between the effectiveness measures on these two vocational goals, moreover, was quite striking. As many as 90 per cent of those who took courses for purposes of job advancement agreed that this was one of the ways the courses had actually helped them. On the other hand, only 57 per cent of those who had enrolled in order to "prepare for a new job or occupation" also identified this as one of the positive consequences resulting from having been enrolled.

One might conclude, then, that vocational education for adults is highly effective when it takes place after one had already entered an occupation or job, but that it is much less effective when its purpose is to lead to initial occupational placement. With regard to this latter function, in fact, the results suggested that when it came to actually finding jobs related to the training received, almost as many participants were unsuccessful in doing so as were successful.

What is not completely clear, however, is whether this occupational placement score indicates a high or a low batting average. Certainly, the task of training adults so they can find new jobs represents a much more difficult assignment than that of extending the skills of people who have already been able to find jobs. Indeed, persons who require vocational training as adults in order to find employment would in large measure be persons in disadvantaged positions vis-a-vis the employment market. Although this group would include some skilled labor force members who were trying to switch from one occupation to another, it would also include large numbers of persons seeking to acquire enough basic skills to be employable in the first place. Thus it is not altogether clear whether the finding that adult education courses were "57 per cent effective" in the function of occupational placement is one which should be interpreted with optimism or pessimism.

III

In this final section of the paper, we will shift our attention away from the actual participants and focus on a wider and somewhat less visible aggregate of individuals—that which might be labeled the potential audience for programs of adult learning.

122

Our first concern in this section will be to trace the extent to which a generalized interest in learning new things is distributed throughout the adult population. Following this, the paper will conclude with some forecasts as to how changes in the composition of the American population are likely to affect the educative behavior of American adults over the next few decades.

Although it would be difficult to outline all of the personal characteristics which make an individual a potential adult education participant, there are at least some general traits which such a person might be expected to possess. We would expect him to reveal an interest in learning more about something; and to display a readiness to do something in order to satisfy these learning interests. Our general thinking about the question of potential audiences for adult education, then, was to view the total adult population as consisting of at least three key aggregates of individuals; first, persons both interested in learning more and favorably disposed toward taking educational courses; second, persons interested in learning new things but who had never considered taking a course; and third, those simply not interested in learning anything at all.

Our main focus in this section, however, will be on the existence of learning interests among adults, and the discussion will therefore consider the very widest possible conception of a potential audience for adult education. In passing we should report that 44 per cent of all adults displayed both a readiness to learn and to take courses; 26 per cent showed an interest in learning but no readiness to take courses; and 29 per cent could not think of anything at all about which they wanted to learn more. Initially, then, we might say that as many as seven adults in ten may have interests which could conceivably make some type of adult learning program relevant to them. Moreover, just under half of the total adult population—an aggregate of perhaps 50,000,000 persons—might be seriously considered as potential participants for adult education courses.

At this point, however, let us examine the question of learning interests more carefully. The actual question which was used to measure the existence of learning interests in the adult population was the following:

Most people have things they'd like to learn more about, or would like to be able to do better. Is there anything in particular that you'd like to know more about, or would like to learn how to do better?

Since the discussion which follows is based on the way this question was answered, we should first clarify what answers to this question probably reflect.

This question was purposely phrased to tap even the barest glimmer of a learning interest if any existed at all, but because of the way it was worded one should not treat positive answers as indications that a person is likely to engage in organized learning pursuits, but rather, that negative answers probably mean rather conclusively that there would be little hope in ever attracting an individual to an adult education program. In effect, then, we are treating the difference between a positive and negative answer to this question as a threshold which differentiates persons who might conceivably be attracted to adult learning programs from those who for all practical purposes would probably never be attracted. The crux of this discussion, of course, rests on the assumption that learning interests represent a necessary (though not sufficient) precondition to participation in adult education studies. The fact that sizable relationships were found between people's previous adult education experiences and the way they answered this question indicated that this assumption might very well be a valid one.[15]

Some additional comments are also in order concerning the distinction between persons who want to learn and persons who take adult education courses. The two aggregates are obviously not the same, and the first way they differ is that only some segment of all those who have things they'd like to learn about actually engage in organized learning pursuits. That the converse is also true—that is, that not all persons who take courses have learning interests—is not quite so obvious since it is tempting to conclude that attendance at a course represents prima facie evidence for the existence of an interest in learning.

On the basis of our earlier discussion, however, there would be good reason to believe that at least some small segment of participants end up taking courses for reasons which have little to do with learning interests.

---

15. "Q" values of association indicated that if we were predicting who had taken part or thought about taking part in educational activities, our predictions would be improved by the following amounts if we knew whether or not a person had current interests in learning something new: (a) by 64 per cent if we were predicting who took an adult education course during the previous five years; (b) by 65 per cent if we were predicting who had engaged in independent self-education during the previous five years; and (c) by 73 per cent if we were predicting who had thought recently about taking an adult education course.

124

It would probably be safe to conclude, in fact, that people who take adult education courses solely to expand their social contacts feel little or no commitment to the subject matter taught in their courses. For these people, participation in any one of a number of activities would probably serve the same function.

This particular segment of adult education participants, of course, is the one which Cyril Houle identifies as the activity-oriented.[16] Houle distinguishes these participants from two other types; the learning-oriented—persons who seek knowledge for its own sake, and the goal-oriented—those who use education in order to accomplish fairly clearcut objectives. Both of these latter types would fall within the aggregate under current discussion since the learning-oriented are obviously interested in learning, while for the goal-oriented an increased knowledge of some subject or skill is seen as a channel to the particular goal they want to accomplish.

There were virtually no differences found between men and women regarding the incidence of an interest in continued learning. However, both age and education had a particularly strong influence on these interests—and in quite predictable directions: learning interests were found to decrease rapidly with increasing age, and to rise just as sharply in the higher educational brackets.

With respect to age, we also found that these interests not only fell off continuously in each succeeding decade, but that the rate of decrease was an accelerating one. The extent of decline was particularly precipitous just after the 40's and then again between the 60's and 70's. Up until the 50's, however, there was no appreciable drop-off in learning interests at all; the rates were only seven per cent higher among persons in their 20's than among those in their 40's (83 per cent compared with 76 per cent).

These results suggested, then, that learning interests are probably affected quite strongly by major life cycle changes, in particular, those which occur at about the time one's children grow up, and again at about the time when people usually retire. The results are not too surprising,

---

16. Cyril O. Houle, The Inquiring Mind (Madison: University of Wisconsin Press, 1961).

since one quite strong attachment an adult can maintain with learning is through the education of his children; and another is in connection with his employment.

The results also showed that education has an equally dramatic impact on learning interests; in fact, the proportion who said there was something they wanted to learn more about jumped from 43 per cent among those with four or less years of schooling to 87 per cent among those who had attended school more than 16 years. And while it was not possible to isolate the exact points in the education continuum when learning interests were most strongly affected, the data did point to a substantial increment of interest when persons were first exposed to a high school education. The peak of interest in learning was reached at about the point of entry into college.

By 1982 the adult population of the United States is going to be considerably larger than it is today. Altogether there will be 150 million adults by then, about 35 per cent more than there were when our inventory was conducted in 1962.[17] A gross increase of one-third over the space of 20 years is an impressive growth rate, but the even more crucial changes as far as the field of adult education is concerned are the additions that will occur within the ranks of younger and better educated adults. While the total population will increase by some 35 per cent over the next 20 years, the increase in the numbers of adults between the ages of 20 and 35 will be much higher than this—in fact, more of the order of a 70 per cent increment in all. In place of a pool of 33,000,000 young adults in 1962, there will be 57,000,000 by 1982.

The changes in the educational characteristics of the adult population will also have a striking impact on the field of adult education. Even very conservative estimates indicate that by 1982 there will be some 59 per cent more adults who have attended high school; and as many as 64 per cent more who have been to college.[18] By contrast, there are likely

17. The figures cover the adult population 20 and over, and are derived from population projections provided by the Bureau of the Census. The population base employed in the computation of estimates in the adult education inventory was slightly larger than the 112 million persons reported here because the earlier estimates included married persons and heads of households who were under 20. The author is indebted to Seymour Sudman for extremely valuable suggestions in the preparation of this section.

18. These estimates were based on the following assumptions: (a)

to be 15 per cent _fewer_ grade-school educated adults in the population. All together, then, there will probably be some 35,000,000 adults who in 1982 will have gone as far as college in their formal education. The crucial point here, of course, is that this represents a social category from which 38 per cent pursued some type of part-time educational activity in 1961-62.

Thus the changes which are going to occur in the composition of the American population over the next two decades are changes which will all work to substantially bolster the categories from which adult education participants most frequently emerge.

In order to estimate the future audiences for adult education, of course, it is necessary to consider the educative practices of future generations of adults as well as the size and composition of the population. However, in the absence of adequate trend data, about the only decision we can make is to assume that rates of activity are going to remain constant over the next couple of decades. This may also be a conservative decision, of course, since there is scattered evidence which suggests that rates of study among persons in specific age and educational categories may be in ascendancy.

In any event, if the 1961-62 rates of participation in adult education are applied to the 1982 estimates of the numbers of men and women in different age and educational categories, a figure of well over thirty million adult education students emerges. Since projections of this sort tend to lack suitable reference points, it seems much more meaningful to emphasize that there will probably be 50 per cent more adult education participants in 1982 than there were in 1962. Between now and 1982, in other words, the number of adult education participants is going to increase at a considerably faster rate than is the total adult population. In this sense, the 1970's and 80's can be designated as decades during which the adult education movement is likely to boom in this country.

The typical adult education participant today is young, urban, and

---

that persons under 35 in the 1982 population will have the same levels of educational attainment as persons under 35 today; (b) that adults who are now 25 years of age or older will not increase their formal educational attainment; and (c) that only a quarter of the population now 55 and over will still be alive in 1982. In view of these, the estimates are on the conservative side.

127

fairly well educated; this is exactly the type of person who will soon be around in greatly increased numbers. Just as in the 50's and 60's, the regular school system had to tool up rapidly to accommodate the greatly increased numbers of young persons in the population, so too in the 70's and 80's the field of adult education will experience increased demands as this population cohort moves into the social categories where greatest use is made of adult education.

Moreover, the prospects for increased numbers of older participants are also very good. More 50, 60, and 70 year-olds will engage in educational pursuits 20 years from now; at that time the average educational attainment of people in these brackets will be considerably higher than it is today. For example, our estimates indicated that by 1982 there will be nearly 3,000,000 less persons 55 and over with only a grade school edcation, and close to 4,000,000 more who have been to college.

What will adult education participants study in 1982? Probably the same general range of subjects as they do today. However, if the increasing amounts of leisure time which have been heralded actually do come to characterize American life by then, the use of adult education in relation to recreational interests will undoubtedly be amplified. On the other hand, the trend toward even greater specialization of occupational skills in our culture shows no prospect of reversal, and in view of this, the much more likely situation is that learning-for-work and learning-for-leisure will together come to dominate the adult education scene to an even greater extent than they do today.

USES OF SOCIOLOGY

The task of establishing sociological foundations for adult education is twofold. First, there is the introduction of relevant sociological data. Second, there are questions related to the use of this knowledge for adult education. Earlier chapters have treated sociology. How may it be used in adult education? At the conference itself each major paper was discussed by analysts who suggested relationships between the two disciplines.[*]

The analysts' comments provide some helpful insights for the adult educator who wishes to apply sociology to his problems, but in no sense are the suggestions intended to be exhaustive. For this volume they serve a more important purpose and that is to propose basic approaches to the examination or application of sociology to adult education. In the papers which follow, the sociological foundations are looked at in three distinct ways: first there are comments on the limitations of sociology for adult education; second, the sociological formulations are applied to the problems of adult education; and finally, there is a wide range of implications which may be drawn from the data.

* * *

In a response to "The Impact of Changing Social Institutions on Adult Life," by Burton Clark, the author is preoccupied almost exclusively with its implications. He comments that the tragedy of human obsolescence is in the field of knowledge, not technology. He believes there is a great need for education for adaptability—and insists the urban population is ready for it.

Irwin Deutscher is an Associate Professor of Sociology and Director of the Youth Development Center, Syracuse University.

---

[*]In some cases respondents did not prepare formal papers for the conference; the papers included in this chapter are by those individuals who actually submitted a manuscript to the editor.

Irwin Deutscher

The central theme of Clark's paper is the dramatic question of human obsolescence. It is the basic theme upon which any number of variations can be played: the problem of automation, the problem of technological unemployment, the problem of retraining, and so on.

These variations do not all have equal relevance to the problems presented in the theme. Technological unemployment, for example, is an old saw; and it is a spurious threat to any society. The historical evidence is overwhelming. The temporary setback in the transition from horse to automobile was minuscule compared with the long range accretion of more and new jobs resulting from that transition. The same is true of the earlier shift of industry from home hand work to factory machine work. Automation is as old as civilization and it has been the key to economic abundance. I am certain that some cave man must have been deeply and sincerely concerned when he first observed the number of strong men who would be left unemployed by the invention of the wheel.

The great tragedy of human obsolescence lies in the field of knowledge rather than the field of technology. It is in the knowledge industries (as Machlup uses the term) where much of the hope for the future lies, and it is precisely in these industries where great investment is most likely to result in bankruptcy. One can learn to operate a machine in a matter of hours or, at most, weeks. To learn to be an engineer or a scientist or a teacher requires the investment of years—not hours or weeks. Yet, as Clark reminds us, rapid developments in the realm of knowledge lead to rapid obsolescence of engineers, scientists, and teachers. College professors too are members of this tragic fraternity. To the extent that he is receiving a good graduate education, in many fields, the graduate student may and frequently does exceed his faculty by the time he receives his doctorate.

The problem of re-training is complex; it is recognized; and it has been and is currently being dealt with on a mass experimental basis. I refer to the federally sponsored re-training projects aimed at miners in West Virginia and Tennessee as well as such locally sponsored efforts as the retraining of knitting mill workers in Utica, New York. The retraining of semi-skilled and skilled workers is probably the least difficult of the great variety of retraining efforts which need to be launched. The problem of learning new techniques is not even problematic when compared with the problem of learning new ways of life which sometimes must accompany those new occupational techniques. For example, the acute nursing shortage following World War II was first approached on a recruiting basis. It soon became obvious that this was a hopeless task in the face of increasing demand not only for nurses but also for a variety of occupational types who were competing for the same young women. The second approach to the nursing shortage resulted in large part from the survey research discovery of large numbers of qualified nurses who were out of the labor market. Retraining programs were initiated and failed dismally. Although there are many reasons for that failure, one of the most significant is that nursing had changed very rapidly, and in more ways than the technical. It was not difficult to update nurses who have been out of practice for a number of years on technical innovations; but it was impossible to re-orient them to the new attitudes of responsibility and authority which were coming to pervade professional nursing. Much the same kind of problem arises in efforts to retrain social workers who have been out of the field for a number of years. The nursing personnel problem was finally solved by introducing new occupational types into the system: the nurses' aid, the practical nurse, the nursing assistant, etc. This solution, incidentally, helped solve another problem—the constructive employment of formerly unskilled and largely unemployable persons.

As Clark implies, the world today changes too fast, the rate of change fluctuates too much, and the directions of change vary like the hues of the rainbow; we simply cannot predict; we cannot project because present factors may be irrelevant in future projections; we cannot distinguish the fads from the fashions from the trends. If we accept this (and I am inclined to), then Karl Mannheim and Burton Clark have formulated the only reasonable beginning to a solution: "The answer, then, is to educate for adaptability, i.e., educate the young to be perceptive and understanding of the social environment and flexible and imaginative in dealing with it, with little control by the patterns of the past." This sounds reasonable and it provides a direction in which to move, but we need much more than that; the words are too pretty and too pat; and just how do we move from such high sounding cliches as "flexible," "imaginative," and "perceptive," to the implementation of the solution? How do we go about accomplishing this thing that sounds so good? And further how do we avoid the concomitant problems of cultural discontinuity and slippage, the creation of extreme individualism—the whole Pandora's Box to which Clark refers. As he says, "The problem is extremely complicated."

We do not, of course, start from scratch: the idea of inevitable, desirable, and necessary change, sometimes referred to as "progress," is essential to the modern urban mentality—just as it was alien to the folk or sacred or rural mentality. If the schools are to educate for adaptability to change they will be doing so within a compatible cultural setting.

A few years ago I was interviewing middle class middle-aged urban Kansas Citians about their life since their children had left home. Taking my cue from the clinicians who had observed that postparental life—that phase of the family cycle following the departure of the last child for work or marriage—was a traumatic and disrupting period for parents whose lives had centered for so many years upon the children, I set out to learn just how awful postparental life really was. I discovered that for most people it was as good or better than any previous stage of the family cycle. One of the important factors which had been overlooked was that urban Americans were imbued with the notion of inevitable change and were prepared to adapt to it no matter whether they had ever experienced anything like it before or not. One mother observed philosophically: "It seems like life spaces itself. You look forward to finishing up one space but then another space always pops up. When this is accomplished something else comes along." A father, unconsciously paraphrasing Shakespeare's scene from As You Like It which begins, "All the world's a stage," explained to me that:

> Of course you hate to give up your daughter, but I think we all understand that is the way of life; you can't stand still; you can't be the same forever. Life moves on and that is the most natural thing. You see them grow. You see them graduate from high school. Then you see them graduate from college—you follow along. It is changing all the time. First it is childhood. You hold them on your lap, then you go walking with them. Then you see them through high school. I was her chauffeur, all the time taking her to social functions. She went through music school, then she got a bachelor of arts, then we sent her for four years to Juilliard and she got her bachelor's and master's there. Then she comes out and teaches in college for one year and then she gets married and settles down.

I think a good many Americans are committed to a philosophy of change and to the extent that this is true the schools have a friendly atmosphere in which to educate for change.

During an era of rapid economic change, Clark reminds us that education has a role "both as a force upon the economy and as an institution which is asked to adjust its own schedules to economic demands." To "adjust" the educational institution to so-called needs defined by outside forces is certainly the easier and more expedient of those two alternatives: however, to react passively to economic whimsy does not reflect responsibility. If brainworkers are the economic need of society, and if it is the awesome responsibility of educators to fill this need, then educators do indeed have a great responsibility and a great deal of influence and, ultimately, power. The first responsibility of the educator is not to fill this need blindly, but to question it. And having assumed the responsibility of questioning the need, the educator may exercise his power by granting or denying its fulfillment. The physicist recognized his responsibility too late—only after he had granted the bomb to the soldier and the politician—because they "needed" it. I think the educator should be reluctant to commit the same error; this is not simply a matter of supply and demand, although the educator can allow it to become one by behaving as if it is.

* * *

In responding to "The Impact of Changing Social Institutions on Adult Life," the author writes primarily from the point of view of an adult educator and suggests four tasks or responsibilities for continuing education. His suggestions are at once applications and implications based on the Clark paper. His four tasks are: (1) a system for exchange and dissemination of new knowledge from research; (2) vocational retraining; (3) education related to values in the face of changing social institutions; and cultural education so vitally needed for life in our contemporary society.

Leonard Freedman is the Head of the Department of Liberal Arts Programs, University Extension, University of California at Los Angeles.

Leonard Freedman

These comments by an adult educator must obviously take up where Burton Clark's paper leaves off: "With adult work being so sharply altered, we are perhaps on the threshold of an age of adult education." I want to underscore this conclusion, and to consider some of the problems it raises.

A massive expansion of the field of adult education is almost certainly to be anticipated as a result of the following factors:

1. In the age of incessant scientific, technological and social change, professional workers cannot rest their development with the completion of formal academic and professional requirements. Research continues implacably in every corner of every field. Clark talks about the periodic retraining that becomes necessary for the engineer and the teacher. It is the same—though perhaps in different ways—for the physicist and chemist, for the doctor, the dentist, the lawyer.

The consequence of this for Extension should not be described simply in terms of communicating research findings to industrial and professional groups outside the university. There are many examples of this kind of thing. But we should not lose sight of the essential fact pointed out by Clark—that the university is not the only center of advanced research today. A great deal goes on in industry, in government, and in quasi-public R and D institutions like the RAND Corporation. It is not even clear that the line between university and non-university research is that between the pure and the applied. There is some rather esoteric research conducted by private industry; and a great deal that is very practical in its application carried on in the university.

So the task of communicating findings from the frontiers of knowledge is not simply a matter of bringing to industry and the community what is happening in the secluded cloisters of the university. The task is to bring about an interchange between those who are farthest along in any area of research, in whatever institutions they are to be found, and those who will have to apply their findings.

Just the same, it is clear that universities are going to have a vitally important place in this process; and university extension agencies will surely have a very large role to play as administrators, as coordinators, as catalysts.

2. Vocational re-training will impose a responsibility of vast proportions on the field of adult education. Clark suggests that "the lower two-

thirds of the occupational structure" will, in time, come to be affected by technological displacement. It is inconceivable that, in fact, adult education institutions could cope with a problem of such dimensions, so that it will be highly necessary for Clark's other prediction to be fulfilled: "We may expect all institutions of work to become more institutions of training."

3. Clark talks about "the slippage in age-old ideals," the possibility that the preoccupation with flexibility may lead to a chaos of values. Thus it would seem to be the role of the university, and of university extension, not only to disseminate new knowledge, but also to ask—how can we cope with it socially, politically, ethically?

This is a question that affects every member of our society and ought to be considered by all of us. However, so urgent are the problems with which we are presented by the surging pace of scientific and technological change that we cannot rely only on programs disseminated to anyone in the general public who will respond. We also have to reach with our extension programs on public policy questions people with key leadership responsibilities in a variety of groups and organizations—business, the professions, the mass media, advertising, public relations, civic organizations, and minority groups. We ought to be involving more scientists and engineers. Clark overstates the case in calling them "the new men of power of the 1950's and 1960's." While it is true that "these are the men whose acts affect our lives," this does not necessarily mean they have controlling decision-making power in a crucial political sense. Still, their expertise does give them influence in problems whose complexity grows more and more baffling for public officials and the general public, so that we should be engaging many scientists and engineers in programs dealing with the implications of their work for the shape and character of our society.

Clark also mentions labor leaders who were, he says, "the new men of power of the 1930's and 1940's." Again, this is too strong a statement. However, there is no doubt that they had more political power then than now; and the persistent undermining of their position is directly attributable to the industrial and technological shifts described in Professor Clark's paper. The labor movement is worried today, and many of the unions are beginning to undertake a fundamental re-appraisal of their situation. University extension agencies could do much more than they are presently doing to help labor equip itself for new functions and responsibilities.

These are illustrations of the kinds of groups who are affected by the dynamic and dislocating forces at large in our society. Many other kinds of organizations and leaders come readily to mind, and it is clear that we must attract them to programs offered by the universities dealing with pressing questions of public responsibility.

We face a difficulty here. I have proposed a crucial job for the university. But who in the university will talk about this kind of thing? Who will ask the basic questions of value?

The problem is that science, or scientism or pseudo-science, is moving in and taking over the very fields in which the questions about science have traditionally been asked.

There are many departments of philosophy in which a majority of the faculty are saying: but we have no particular competence to speak on moral and value questions. Our job is to refine the tools of thought and analysis—a scientific, even mathematical task. Thus it becomes difficult to find a philosopher who will deal frontally with the great contemporary issues.

To a considerable extent this is becoming true of the social sciences, where quantification and methodology have become the preoccupation of a large number of scholars.

It is this, together with the increasing specialization of our universities, that leads people like Robert Hutchins to argue that the university environment is essentially hostile to liberal education. Hutchins says that scientism has become dominant, and that the development of moral and intellectual virtues can only come about if we "build intellectual communities outside the American educational system."[1] I do not think we should write off the universities as yet. The trend toward scientism is there, but

---

1. Robert M. Hutchins, et al., Science, Scientists and Politics, Center for the Study of Democratic Institutions, 1963, p. 4.

it has not taken over completely. Encroachments in philosophy are serious; but it is still possible to embark on a career in any one of several branches of the social sciences without possessing a mastery of mathematics. There also exist historians and teachers of literature and the classics who will talk about human values.

So the task of staffing programs dealing with the broad implications of the outpouring of new knowledge described by Clark is growing more difficult, but it has not become impossible for us.

4. There is little doubt but that rising levels of education and affluence, together with increasing leisure, is leading toward a great expansion of the public for the arts and other cultural activities. All of the well-known indices of paper-back sales, concert attendance, and so on, point to the fact that the cultural explosion is already upon us; and the financial estimates are that the market in this respect may almost triple between now and 1970.

Not all of this will represent pure gain in American cultural life. There will be much that is precious and status-seeking about it. Moreover, the expansion of the cultivated minority does not as yet seem to be having much effect on the quality of the majority culture. The amount of mediocrity on television and elsewhere remains staggeringly high; and the triumphant statistics on attendance and sales in the arts may hide in the future a deep and growing schism between the minority which loves the arts and the life of the mind, and the majority which does not.

There are, then, immensely disquieting elements in this picture, for the assumption of a democratic society is that standards of excellence will be widely diffused and not become the preserve of an elite. Just the same, for adult education, and for university adult education especially, the minority of adults that clamors to be educated in the arts is a very large one and its growth will extend our resources to their limits.

We are likely to encounter, then, a massive growth of the adult education audience. But the problem for our own profession is not simply one of quantity. If we are to acquit ourselves well in dealing with the tasks which I have indicated—professional development, vocational retraining, education for public responsibility, education in the arts—we shall have to raise our own professional standards constantly.

In part this will lead to an increasing emphasis on higher degrees. But the crux of the problem is not to have more and more people in adult education with doctorates, though this will undoubtedly be the case. The essential point is that we must have among our number more people who have an understanding of the changes described by Clark, and of their larger consequences for society; who have a love for the arts and for ideas; who have a substantive background in one of the major fields of intellectual inquiry and yet are generalists, capable of engaging in the reconstruction and integration of ideas for the broader public.

My impression is that the process of attracting more people to our field who have the qualifications needed to cope with these pressing responsibilities is already well under way. But there is much more to be done if we are to keep pace with the general rise in educational standards and professional qualifications which is a key fact of the new age described by Professor Clark.

* * *

In his response to "Changing Status and Roles in Adult Life Cycles," Stern concentrates the limitations of the research and then suggests some implications for adult education. Writing from the point of view of a teacher of particular students, the author objects to the generalized nature of social roles and emphasizes individual differences. At the same time he recognizes the significance of the generalization in identifying the deviations and further suggests that social roles developed by Havighurst for adult education need to increase the adults generativity and to prepare him for wise use of leisure time.

Bernard Stern is the Associate Dean, School of General Studies, Brooklyn College.

Bernard H. Stern

Adult education in America today is, in the view of the educator, either for credit or non-credit. The studies which are undertaken by adults for credit lead to a degree or certificate; non-credit work is generally sporadic and undertaken for immediate pleasure or profit. The relevance of Dr. Havighurst's paper is more to the non-credit rather

138

than the credit type of adult education in that it delineates changes in status and role induced in the adult mainly by biological forces. In my opinion, adults who attend college for credit seek to induce such changes in status and roles by their own efforts.

My experience has been chiefly in adult education for credit, more specifically in the Brooklyn College Degree Program for Adults (1). In this program life experience is equated with college credit and adults are afforded an enriched and accelerated curriculum. With a background of experience with such adults, I shall speak to Havighurst's paper from the point of view of the adult educator concerned with study for credit.

Although the paper contains lucid definitions of changing adult roles, it is too schematic and generalized to form a sound basis for the structuring of curricula in adult education. The impression produced by the paper is almost fatalistic, with changes preordained by mainly biological and sometimes social forces as people grow older: "At 50 libidinal forces[*] begin to die down; at 60 his colleagues expect him to slow down."

From my experience with adults as students I should hesitate to attribute specific characteristics or tendencies to age groups. I rather prefer to look at an adult as Personality A or B or C, in whom changes are noted not so much because of biological forces but because of life experience:

A man, age 50, now president of a large national chain of retail drug stores, had studied pharmacy briefly in 1926. He had 28 years of experience as buyer and manager in various merchandising enterprises. He had been chairman of numerous large scale fund raising campaigns of philanthropic organizations and was a trustee of a college of pharmacy. Thoroughly versed in business and finance, he was motivated to earn a college degree at this stage in his life by the desire to "teach young people at the college level the skills and knowledge acquired over a life-time in the business world." In this man there was hardly a decline of strength or skill, nor was there any interference with the operation of his ego as described in Havighurst's paper.

It is difficult to see how so sharp a distinction can be made between

---

[*]Havighurst states that by this phrase he meant "sexual activity." I interpreted it to mean "psychic energy."

instrumental and expressive forms of education. The motivation of an adult for education may be "non-vocational," but he finds the education to be of practical value not merely in promotion on the job but in the heightened esteem that he may command from his family and friends. By the same token, instrumental education can, by skillful teaching, be made so interesting and enjoyable that it takes on the characteristics of expressive education. I believe that learning can only be really successful if it is pleasurable; that is, if libidinal forces are at work.

The description of "Age 30-40," entitled "collecting one's energies" is extremely generalized and subject to so many exceptions that it is often not a true picture. Such statements as "The mother has her children and rears them with relative ease and pleasure," "Doubts about oneself have been put to rest . . . and the situation is generally stable and satisfactory," or "This is a period of . . . freedom from anxiety and general psychological well-being" are very sweeping. The implication is that the person who at age 20 is emotionally torn, is at age 30 psychologically at ease. My experience has been that this is not so. Many adults were, in their 20's relatively at ease, since they were often still single, without responsibilities, and supported by their parents. In their 30's, however, they were faced with stresses arising out of marriage, children, jobs, and financial problems. The young mother of an infant, who is likely to be in her 20's, enjoys caring for the helpless infant who needs her so much, while she might be quite stressed emotionally taking care of that same child 12 years later when she is in her 30's and he is a rebellious, aggressive adolescent.

It seems to me that there is too much emphasis in the paper on the biological regressive changes of middle age. A wise man becomes wiser as he grows older; a limited man becomes more limited. In my interviews with adults seeking a college education I have observed large numbers between 40 and 60 in whom there was no slackening of drive or "abandonment of developmental tasks." A fireman was preparing himself to be a minister after his retirement; a successful business man wanted in middle age to become a teacher of music. Many middle aged adults thus seek a change of role but not because of slackening of drive, perhaps rather because of increased drives, now that these drives are unhampered by responsibilities of small children, with resulting financial and emotional stresses.

It is not true in my experience that people tend to drop out of adult education activity by the age of 40. In the Brooklyn College Degree Program for Adults a large number of the applicants for admission have been between 40 and 60. Most of them have expressed a desire for personal fulfillment. They wanted to make up in adulthood what they had missed in youth. They felt that there were gaps in their knowledge and understanding which they sought to fill in. The possession of a college education represented to them a source of personal satisfaction and a broadening of their interests.

To say that "libidinal fires" are dying at age 50 similarly does not coincide with what I have observed. Large numbers of adults 50 and older have great reserves of psychic energy. If the statement were true, how would we account for the effectiveness of our Presidents, of Popes, of such statesmen as De Gaulle, Adenauer and Churchill, or of Frank Lloyd Wright, Robert Frost and Bertrand Russell?

As a whole, Havighurst's paper presents generalizations or "norms" which are useful in measuring the deviations from them of adults who seek formal education. A large number of them are deviants in this sense (2).

Of the dominant concerns of adults which suggest centers of emphasis for a program of adult education, the most important are the achievement of generativity and integrity between ages 40 and 60 (3). To give the best of one's self to continue to improve human life and human society and to accept one's life as worthwhile and as something one can take pride in, it is necessary for an adult to immerse himself, under guidance, in the large issues contained in the humanities, sciences, and social sciences, thus becoming familiar with the promises, failures, and successes of modern knowledge in understanding the human condition. This is one of the major aims of the Brooklyn College Degree Program which we try to achieve through a curriculum built around special adult seminars in the major fields of knowledge. A program of serious study of this kind can capitalize on the dominant concerns of ages 40-60 and can facilitate role changes that lead to increased effectiveness and happiness.

In the area of non-credit adult education the most important developmental task to be considered is that of making wise and satisfying use of leisure time.

141

The apprehension with which the effects of automation upon the individual are viewed stems from the notion that the age of automation may deprive the individual of his accustomed outlets for individual expression by (a) increasing non-work time, which is "unproductive" because it is not "employed" usefully, and (b) stereotyping and regimenting the culture in which he lives by imposing automated uniformity in the processes of production, distribution, and consumption, thus radically reducing the areas of individual preference, standards, and taste and hastening the tendency toward regimentation, robot-like, of mind, heart, and spirit.

That this apprehension is unrealistic may be observed in the results of earlier technological progress which made possible increased production and wider distribution of the material comforts of life and shortened the working day. Clothing workers in New York City in 1915 worked in sweat shops some sixteen hours a day, six or seven days a week. Today, organized in labor unions, they work only seven hours a day, five days a week. They not only have more of the necessities of life but more leisure time, and they are encouraged and guided through lectures, museum trips, theaters, concerts, garden visits, sports and recreational activities, travel, and formal education. The clothing workers of today are richer, finer personalities than their predecessors of fifty years ago because they have leisure time and opportunities to channel their creative energies into activities far more pleasurable and enriching than sweat shop production. Their individual lives are healthier, happier, fuller, and, in the social sense, more fruitful because they are better informed, better motivated, and more insightful and discriminating as citizens and as human beings.

When questioned recently as to what they would do with increased leisure time, most factory workers replied that they would "work around the house" or "spend more time with the family." Some responded that they might travel or engage in spectator or activity sports. A few said they would read, go to school, or obtain an additional job. The least number of responses showed possible interest in social, fraternal, civic, and religious organizations. This is a sorry picture of the present state of enlightenment on the part of our workers concerning channels for the satisfying expenditures of time and energy and for the attainment of an adequate identity (4).

If we are to preserve the individual in an age of automation, such enlightenment must be made available on the largest possible scale so that the quality of our American culture may be raised and the happiness and individual fulfillment of our people enhanced. A recent study of continuing education in America made by the National Opinion Research Center (5) revealed that during the period from June 1, 1961, to June 1, 1962, about 17 million adults were enrolled in some continuing education course or activity. About 9 million more were engaged in some form of systematic independent self-education and about 2-1/2 million were enrolled as full-time students. An adult was defined in the study as anyone either 21 or over, or married, or the head of a household. The estimated total adult population, so defined, was 114 million, so that those engaged in continuing education represented about one-quarter of American adults. Continuing education was defined as the activity transferring systematic learning processes to the interests and needs of adult life, and the major stress in this kind of education was found to be practical rather than academic, emphasizing skills and information leading to better living.

The forms of instruction included classes, lecture series, discussion groups, private lessons, on-the-job training, television courses, as well as various other formats. Independent self-instructional activities involved the individual in consciously and systematically organizing a program of study for himself and following it for a period of not less than one month. About half of the subjects studied were in the categories of vocational, agricultural, home and family life, and personal development. About 27 per cent of the courses were in the academic, religious, and public affairs categories. About 3-1/2 million adults were studying such general education subjects as foreign languages, mathematics, literature, history, psychology, social sciences, and great books. Sponsoring agencies included churches, colleges, community organizations, business and industry, public and private schools, government, and the armed forces.

Herein lies the hope for the preservation of the individual in an age of automation. In continuing education people study the good things of life with mature interest. For them Homer, Dante, and Shakespeare are not dull, and they find profound meaning in the ideas of the great masters of human thought and creation. They are not impatient of poetry and art and philosophy because they are not motivated vocationally and thus are not pressed by society's concern with the practical, the useful, and the quickly obtained.

143

Leisured people are the ideal students in a democracy. As taxpayers, parents, voters, and occupants of a specific social status, they know the present and part of the past. They are aware of the complexities of life. They desire enrichment and deeper understanding. They need to measure their values against the best of man's thoughts and deeds. They need to ask: Who decides what is important for me—my relatives, my friends, my society, or I myself? What criteria determine what is important for me—personal satisfaction, curiosity, pleasure and comfort, my service and contribution to my fellow man, spiritual and emotional growth, creative stimulus, social prestige, fame, a sense of freedom and enlargement? What ethical and moral considerations should enter into my values —honesty, integrity, loyalty, love, conformity, courage, perseverance, independence, initiative? What rewards and satisfactions do my values bring—money, peace of mind, happiness, good will, physical ease and comfort, excitement and thrills, a sense of self-fulfillment?

The individual who channels his creative energy into continuing education finds dignity and worth in himself as a person by the exercise of his mind, imagination, and sensibilities in ways that make him a fuller, more cultured, and more interesting personality.

References

1. Stern, Bernard H., Never Too Late for College, Chicago, CSLEA, 1963.

2. Stern, Bernard H., Adults That Grew in Brooklyn and Some That Didn't, Chicago, CSLEA, 1963.

3. Erickson, Erik H., Childhood and Society, New York, Norton, 1950.

4. Stern, Bernard H., Preserving the Individual in An Age of Automation, not yet published.

5. Johnstone, John, Learning for Living, Chicago, 1962.

* * *

Russell Smith, ostensibly responding to Eugene Friedmann, actually directs his comments to limitations shared by sociologists and adult educators alike. He is concerned about three confusions generally held by both groups: (1) education from the cradle to the grave; (2) the Madison Avenue approach to sales and promotion of adult education; and (3) the dichotomizing of education into liberal versus vocation, instrumental versus expressive, and so on.

Russell F. W. Smith is Associate Dean at the Division of General Education and Extension Services, New York University.

Russell F. W. Smith

It is hard to know whether an adult educator should be encouraged or driven to despair to discover that the sociologists and the education sociologists, when they sharpen their social-scientific tools to dissect the (still-living) body of adult education, are just as confused as the adult educators—and over much the same problems or questions. For better or for worse that is one of the strongest impressions I am left with after reading the papers prepared in advance by Professor Friedmann and others and after hearing the discussion at this conference.

To enumerate, if not to rank, the confusions we share, let me label as Confusion #1 the Cradle-to-the-Grave, 100-Percent-Audience Confusion. No confusion, of course, is so simple and clear as labeling and describing can make it seem; live, it comes infected with the barnacles, tapeworms, or body-lice of subproblems and cohabiting with other problems (either incestuous or otherwise unrelated), frequently of oddly assorted size. You meet the 100-Percent Confusion in clinical isolation, however, when you hear the adult educator boasting about the recidivist who has been taking courses at his school for 35 years, or worrying because despite all he hears about increased leisure time and early retirement, he does not get many students over 65. The frequently unexamined assumptions are of course, that it is good for anybody to keep coming to adult education courses and that it would be better if everybody did. Professor Havighurst and Friedmann both seem to worry about this in much the same way that many adult educators do and, in fact, conclude that the fact that there is something very wrong with adult education is proved by Johnstone's figures that show far less common participation in adult education by people over 50.

I should not like to be considered a complacent defender of the status quo of university adult education; there are too many things wrong with every university program of continuing education to justify complacency. But I should like us to be sure we worry about the right things. Until some years pass and then only we are fortunate enough to have a replication of the N.O.R.C. study so that it can be seen whether there is an increase or a decrease in the percentage of people over 50 participating in adult education and how that increase or decrease compares with those shown by other age-groups, we shall have no clear statistical implication that adult education is particularly remiss in meeting its obligations to

145

older adults. To be sure, it is only too likely that we are not planning the right courses for the new leisured and retired classes, just as we are not planning the right courses for other people. But before we devote our full frenetic energies to course-planning and recruiting for this age-group, we will do well to consider a question the 100-Percenters pass lightly by. Do we not have a responsibility, not unlike the therapist's, to avoid developing in adult education students an endless dependency—should we not be concerned with people's becoming self-educating so that, sooner or later, they will be free of us and come back to us only for new personal or career needs, new education crises large or small (occupational retraining, professional updating, new personal curiosities) that they have not learned how to meet by themselves. Ultimately, continuing education may be able to pride itself on how many older people do not need to come back to school.

I assure you that we have not yet reached that prideful day. We almost certainly have today too many people who need the adult education we offer, but do not want it and do not know that they need it (recruitment). We also offer too few of the things that are needed (programing) at the time when they are needed (timing—otherwise to be defined in adult education as successful recruitment resulting from good programing, as distinct from recruitment through advertising ingenuity). To consider what can be done to improve programing (not only for older adults, but for all adults), the adult educator will do well to ponder the concepts of adult life cycles, of changing status and roles of adults, of changing value-orientations that Professors Havighurst and Friedmann have discussed, but we must not expect or settle for too superficial or simplistic solutions. Professor Friedmann perhaps is suggesting such inadequate guides to programing when in the "case study" with which he concludes, he says of a four-week adult residential seminar surveying the relationship between scientific and humanistic thought over the last 400 years, "Although no mention was made of its appropriateness for the older adult, it was felt that persons would be attracted who are presently stressing leisure rather than work objectives . . . " and infers that the feeling was correct from the fact that more than half those enrolled were over 50. The subject matter of the seminar could just as well have made it especially appropriate as part of the job-training—pardon me, executive development—of the administrators of certain business concerns, if the seminar had been so conceived and so promoted. The fact that over half the registrants were over 50 is far more likely to be related to the seminar's being full-time for four weeks (too long a time for most adults before 50 because of their job, family, and community involvements) than to its subject matter.

The second confusion that I have found in this Conference on Sociological Backgrounds of Adult Education as well as in meetings of the Association of University Evening Colleges and the National University Extension Association is the Madison-Avenue Confusion of recruitment or promotion or salesmanship with programing. The Madison-Avenuers are hypnotized by their sales charts or enrolment statistics into a confusing of means and ends that results in offering only what easily gets large enrolments and concentrates on maximizing sales by minimizing sales resistance. The consequences are likely to be homogenized and tasteless bread, beer, and courses that nobody wants unless loud singing commercials imprint our audience with our institutions' slogans and images. We are not unaware as adult educators that we live part of the year on Madison Avenue—we remind ourselves of the dangers in the private reaches of the night and we remind each other at national conferences—and it should not have surprised us to have several of the sociologists in the discussion periods scold us for a Television—or Hollywood-like habit of selling our public short by programing down to a common denominator in the mass-media delusion that this is programing to "reach people where they are" or to "give them what they want."

Certainly a consideration of what sociologists and educational sociologists know or suspect about adults should help keep the adult educator off Madison Avenue. But at this conference, it has seemed to me that the sociologists move there too when they talk about adult education. Not only do they judge from the sales figures (not enough customers over 50), but they show a tendency to program the easily salable. A consideration of life-cycles and changing needs will not help us much if we adopt an oversimplified "readiness" or "developmental task" notion as the basis for programing. We can end up on Madison Avenue, that way too. Professor Friedmann, for example, in discussing "Stage 4" of the "family career" of a woman, says, "the time orientation (during widowhood) would be Present or perhaps Past. . . . Adult education in this first instance would be able to offer participation in hobbies and crafts . . . direct satisfaction. . . . In the second instance of Past orientation local history might be of interest to a long time resident of an area." This smacks far too much of

the let's-be-sure-that-we-stock-the-right-impulse-goods-so-that-we-
have-good-point-of-purchase-sales attitude. What we need to learn from
Professor Friedmann—and can learn from his paper—is the need to examine people's lives and our programs so that our programing is deeply,
not point-of-purchase superficially, relevant to their various careers.
Instead of crash therapy of hobbies and crafts for idle widows, we need
to examine what role continuing education can have and what role it
should have in reshaping the careers that otherwise run down and in en-
couraging the development of alternate or even conflicting careers not
on an emergency basis after the crisis but in preventive anticipation of
the crisis. It is too easy for us—or for the sociologists—to think we have
done something good and sufficient if we get people enrolled (our terminology) or involved (theirs).

A third confusion that adult educators seem to share with sociologists is a philosophical or semantical confusion of the How-Do-I-Know-
What-I'm-Doing sort. Despite their professional deformations that necessarily and usefully prescribe a certain detachment and objectiveness
about what they do as programers and operators of adult education or
what they do as observers and describers of, or experimenters with, society, adult educators and sociologists alike have a tendency to sort out
different motives for adult education (vocational vs. liberal arts, individual vs. community, instrumental vs. expressive, extrinsic vs. intrinsic,
etc.), and to make at once too much and too little of the versus. As Professors Havighurst and Friedmann both pointed out during discussion,
the oppositions are trial hypotheses for the sake of analysis—does it make
sense to make this particular distinction even though actual motivations
are always mixed. It may be that the evidence at this conference is that
the distinction is worse than useless, actually harmful. At least there
was a tendency, passim in papers and in discussion, simply to accept the
dichotomy (making too much of the versus) and then to take all examples
from instrumental motivation for education relevant to work careers and
life careers, paying little attention to other careers or other motivations
until at times to a Martian observer we must have seemed not a conference on the sociological backgrounds of adult education, but a conference
on retooling hourly workers three times in a lifetime (making too little of
the versus).

I disagree with Professor Friedmann's proposition that participation

148

in adult education programs is related to the degree of compatibility between the orientations of the program and the value orientations of its participants or at least do not consider the relationship of much significance because in fact many adults do participate, even enthusiastically, in incompatible programs and because a difference in orientation (to be sure it should be a difference short of complete incompatibility) is presumably essential if education is going to take place—assuming that education does and can involve deliberate attention to "value-orientations" and to changing them. It presumably would be invaluable to have more attempts to conduct research, whether by adult educators or by educational sociologists or by both, to determine what effects adult education has or can have on value-orientations.

The chief value to adult educators of Professor Friedmann's paper, like that of Professor Havighurst's, it seems to me is the possibility that the concepts and terminology employed will lead to further attempts more successfully to relate programing in adult education to the real lives and the real needs of actual and potential adult students. I hope, however, that the split between "instrumental" and "expressive" will not lead us to suppose that we program for a man in two separate stages of his life or for his careers as worker and as player as if he were two chronologically distinct though related species (homo laborans and homo ludens). I prefer to hope that our concern with man's "expressiveness" and with the inadequacies of his career as worker and his career as family man (because ambitions succeed or fail, retirement comes, children grow up, sex palls, and spouses die) to fill his life-space with satisfaction will result in our having a stronger commitment than ever before to man's career as a human individual (homo cogitans), variously involved at various times but always committed to at least one kind of interest (perhaps professional, perhaps extra-professional, but never merely recreational) that will last as long as life and reason and feeling. This is, I think, what some people are calling for when they stress the importance of a "general liberal education" or when they say that what this country needs is more amateurs —"amateurs in the best sense of the word." We need a minimum, I suggest.

Presented as a response to "America's Adults in the Sixties," the author suggests limitations and implications of demographic statistics. She warns adult educators that statistics are predicated on normal events and cannot provide for any serious deviations. Sheldon's predictions imply a necessity for drastic changes in educational institutions which she finds sadly inflexible and conservative.

Blanche Geer is a Research Associate, Community Studies, Inc., Syracuse University.

Blanche Geer

Sheldon has given us what I would like to call a well-balanced view of our present population and what it may be in 1970. Because he is so well aware of the complicated interdependencies of statistical data he gives what may seem a conservative picture. Census data are so often used to rationalize the wishes of an institution or group, and taken out of context and perhaps unconsciously falsified in the process, that the balanced perspective he has given us is a wonderful corrective.

Our 1970 population will not be startlingly different from that of 1960, he says, but at the same time suggests that several long-term trends will probably continue into the next decade. I would like to enter one reservation to Sheldon's facts and figures; one of which he is well aware and scarcely responsible for. Population prediction on the basis of long-term trends can be dramatically wrong sometimes, although it may more often prove right. It proves dramatically wrong, and trends are reversed, when events (which we later call history) change social structure, human actions, and values—I am thinking of wars, depressions, and revolutions, racial or otherwise. The statistician bases his projections on an absence of such major upheavals. He bets that they will not occur. But, as we know, they do. It seems to me likely that the revolution presently going on in our Negro population, depending upon its outcome, may change the figures in the 1970 census in ways that neither Sheldon nor anyone else can predict. Nevertheless, I am going to try to take this revolution into account in relation to education. My comments will not be based on any magnificent array of figures, but on a shaky base of scattered reading, allied research, and what I could dignify as sociological concepts of social change, but might more rightly call a feeling for the way the winds of social change can blow. Let me give you a set of possibilities bred of private, quasi-professional speculation.

150

Sheldon has given us data on many sectors of our population, but I think changes in three of the groups he has discussed are relevant to education: the young married population, women, and the labor force.

What do Sheldon's projections imply for schools and colleges?

The peripheral areas of the country will continue to be driven by pressures for more teachers, more classrooms, more money to finance education. Central city schools, while they will have less and less of a problem with children of immigrant groups who do not speak English and without adequate knowledge of American ways, will continue to face the problems of an incoming group from relatively impoverished areas of our country whose notions of the English language and school manners are at variance with those of city populations. Some city school systems will react to this continuing pressure with improved and novel ways to help these children. Other school systems which have managed up to now to ignore questions of racial imbalance and the difference in the type and quality of education offered in slum and suburban schools will find they must solve these problems as more and more people come to see them as intolerable, and un-American, inequities.

We do not know whether the current protest of the Negro will explode into further and more general violence or whether his peaceful, if not always legal, methods of demanding his rights will continue. I will hazard a guess that during the next decade the Negro will continue his emphasis upon education as his most basic right. It is a passport to a promised land of human dignity. But the bitter struggle simply to get in white schools is only the first phase of the battle. Once it is won, the fighters will not be satisfied with the stultifying, frequently meaningless routine of some of our schools. They will want schooling which truly educates and prepares their children for a modern world.

During the last decade we have seen a drive for excellence in the schools spread through the upper strata of our white population. A higher and more serious brand of education is demanded; there must be reforms in the training of teachers, rapid innovation in teaching methods, modernization of the operation of entire school systems. We are no longer in the stage of simply being pleased with ourselves for offering education to millions. We have embarked upon a period of demanding that the best education we are capable of be offered to everybody, regardless of residential district, income or race. The combined pressure of whites and Negroes for better education will inspire some school systems to innovate, to reach out for help outside their own discipline and into the community in raising the quality of education. I think that in many school systems the coming decade will therefore be an exciting one for teachers and administrators, and probably even some of the children. There should be a sense of movement and change. Teaching may even become a desirable career.

Other school systems, which have not yet begun to move under the pressures of immigration and racial imbalance, will have a difficult time. Stubborn administrators with closed minds, half-educated teachers without the imagination to innovate, will be unhappy and incapable of making the necessary changes which they may well feel are being forced upon them from the outside. Such school systems, I would predict, will find it increasingly difficult to get high-level teachers. There will be other places to teach and administer which will be full of innovation and excitement, and this is one of the chief things that attracts teachers. It is not simply salaries or polite middle-class students, but the opportunities to make significant contributions that are offered by rapidly-changing social structures. We may well find that we will have in our country a sharp division within the next ten years, in which quite a large number of school systems which have utilized the pressures toward change attract the best people, while other school systems become increasingly intolerable, backward, and strife-torn. I am not speaking here of the schools in the South, but of the schools in the country as a whole. Under the pressure for change, I think that the pattern of rather good and innovative schools in the wealthy suburbs and poor schools in central city and rural areas will break down, and we will find that the best school systems may well be those where there has been the strongest pressure for change together with a willingness to undertake it.

Sheldon throws out an interesting idea about the development of metropolitan areas in the near future. He suggests that we may no longer think in terms of central city vs. suburb as devices of metropolitan government are developed. I think it would be visionary to suppose that radical changes will be made in the organization of school systems within the next ten years—that is, I doubt if we will get to the point of having metropolitan-wide school systems or will break away from the tradition of local school boards. There may well be movement in this direction, however, in the increasing pressure to avoid racial imbalance and the need to transfer students from one school to another.

I have been speaking largely of children in the elementary and high school years. But Sheldon gives us a number of predictions about what the population in 1970 will be like, which will drastically affect our colleges and make still more obvious some of the trends already in force. He mentions several long-term trends that will probably mean a continued pressure upon the colleges to expand the quantity of students they educate, if not the quality of education they offer. The children of the expanding professional group will continue to head for college as the children of professionals have in the past, and there will be many more of them during the next decade. There will be more interest in the academic type of high school preparation, more interest in going to college, more interest in graduate work, and increases in income will make college more possible for more people.

The continued trend of women into the labor force (if I may return for a moment to the public schools) and the increasing number of young married women who work should put still further demands on the schools to expand their services to young children and to take still more responsibility for all children for longer periods of time during the day. The trend we have already witnessed toward an increased responsibility on the part of the school for supervision of extracurricular activities, recreation, and morals of their pupils, will continue. (This trend, incidentally, has been little mentioned of late in the great furor about increasing the academic quality of the schools. I have no reason to suppose that pressures upon the schools to take more and more responsibilities for larger areas of children's lives is not continuing underneath the protest, however. Lessening responsibility in the home, if only because the parents are not there to exercise it, and the lessening power of church and other agencies in children's lives, leaves the school in charge. Some of the recent agitation about regulation of dress in the high schools is a good example.)

But the increasing number of working mothers will have perhaps an even more startling affect on the colleges. We should witness a slowly increasing demand from women for an education which will prepare them for specific jobs and a wider range of jobs than they have heretofore been interested in. I think that there will be an increasing tendency for women to feel that they should use what education they have in work. The colleges will face demands for relaxation of their rigid and over-formalized requirements for four years of undergraduate residence, for courses with many and particular prerequisites, and the many regulations with which students on a residential campus are able to comply but which are out of the question for women with families who live at a distance from the campus. Many colleges make little or no provision for such people. Other colleges have long been involved in adult education programs which open their classes to part-time students and make it possible to get part-time degrees. But this is more frequent in metropolitan areas than elsewhere. I think that this greater flexibility and re-examination of some of the rules and regulations now in force will become necessary if the colleges are to accommodate the women who want higher education.

Furthermore, universities will have to think through some of their present shibboleths. I know of a woman of 40 with an excellent academic record who was refused entrance to a Ph.D. program in English solely on the basis of age. Practically without exception women over 35 are turned down by medical schools. The increasing trend for relatively young women to return to work after their children have left home should force the colleges to look at their notions about age more carefully. The present life expectation of women is so great that even an academic program of ten years, if embarked upon in the 40's, would leave many years of working life after completing a degree.

The continuing trend of families to have children at a younger age, and to have their last child leave home when they are still young, should accelerate this pattern. Perhaps what I am saying is more in the nature of a hope rather than a prediction. Women are much more modest in their demands than other minority groups have been. They do not think of themselves, in fact, as a group with minority status in education. This is partly because women have had the opportunity to attend most colleges for many years. They have had the opportunity, however, provided they fit in with the pattern of continuous attendance established in the past for young males. If Sheldon is correct in saying that the trend toward more and more women in the labor force will continue, it is probable that women will speak up more for themselves in demanding the relaxation of requirements which make it difficult for them to get a college education.

154

The third trend which Sheldon emphasized in his paper is one which is presently getting almost as much attention in our newspapers and from our national, state and local governments as the race issue, in part because it is connected with race. The Secretary of Labor believes that by the 1970's it will be necessary for adults in all occupations, not just blue collar occupations, but the professions as well, to re-train themselves three times during their working lifetime. The old pattern of becoming educated for one job and working at this throughout one's life is apparently coming to an end. For industrial and white collar jobs automation is bringing about the change. In the professions, rapidly accumulating scientific knowledge makes it necessary for the scientist, teacher and researcher to master new fields which may not have even been heard of at the time he obtained his first professional degree. In our most advanced scientific disciplines, the time has come when great fusions take place between one discipline and another. There are increasing numbers of hyphenated disciplines and hyphenated degrees where the graduate student is required to master at least two fields. For the very bright students in the very best universities the straight course in one discipline is becoming less and less frequent as the good ones are urged out into the new combined fields. Apparently when a certain accumulation of scientific knowledge has taken place, tremendous advances occur by a seeding process from another discipline. At the present time people with a degree in one field and experience in another are now most in demand. I don't think that many of our graduate schools have reacted to this pressure as yet, or at least they have done little to organize themselves to further this type of education, but there will be increasing pressure upon them to do so.

The industrial and blue collar occupations have already forced themselves upon the consciousness of educators. The government is this year instituting a nation-wide program in the re-training of workers; much of this is going on outside the regular school system, which has in many instances, been unable to cooperate in developing new programs or expanding its facilities to meet the need. There is a reawakened interest in vocational education and in particular in methods of training people for the jobs that there are, and in obtaining more knowledge through research of the relationship of economic demand to the education of our labor force. It is no longer possible for the schools to close their eyes, as they have done in the past, to the needs of the economy for people with particular

155

training. There is a tremendous shortage of technical workers, but very few schools or programs to train them. There is an incredible lack of knowledge in the schools about the actual skills and demands of various occupations. On the whole, the schools have attempted to meet the question of demand from the labor market without adequate knowledge of what is going on. For instance, in a given year it will be publicized that there is a shortage of engineers. Thereupon, counselors and advisors head high school and college students into courses to supply this demand; but by the time they graduate, the need is over if it ever developed, and there is a shortage in some other field. The government is taking a number of steps toward greater understanding of the demands of industry and its relationship to education, and I should expect these to bear fruit in the coming decade with increasing pressures upon the public school systems, the junior colleges, the colleges and graduate schools, to train people for the jobs that are needed and retrain them when their skills become obsolescent. These demands and pressures being brought by the government (and I don't think there is any doubt that such pressures would continue under a Republican as well as a Democratic administration as long as there is a high level of unemployment) open up a tremendous new area for innovation and change in our present schools. The problem of training workers for the jobs we have, and retraining those with inadequate skills or unwanted skills, is closely allied to the racial crisis and its urgency is magnified by the connection. The schools have scarcely made a beginning in these areas, but I should expect a proliferation of innovation and expansion during the coming decade.

The very strong pressures and demands that seem to me to flow from the moderate, well-considered predictions of Sheldon suggest that the coming decades will be a period of rapid change, innovation, upheaval, and in some areas, failure and disorganization in our schools. It will also be, as I have suggested earlier, an exciting period. The old rigidities must fall if we are to solve some of these more and more urgent problems. I recently attended a meeting in New York City called to pool information about the problems of central city slum schools, and what can and ought to be done about them. While there was an awareness on the part of teachers and administrators that something ought to be done, it was quite obvious from the tenor of the meetings that the various entrenched political power systems would present almost insuperable barriers to any but the smallest changes. A man from the Department of Labor spoke, saying that the schools were so slow-moving and so rigid in the city that he believed they would have to be side-stepped in the tremendous drive his Department is putting on for vocational education and retraining of the unemployed. This angered the school people; they said in their Republican way that this was another evidence of the impracticality of Democratic Washington. But politics aside, it suggested a possibility to me which would be dramatic indeed. It may be that our school systems are too entrenched and too rigid to change quickly enough to do some of the things that people increasingly want them to do. Under these circumstances I believe the pressures for change will be great enough for new forms of educational institutions to grow up side by side with the schools.

At the meeting on slum schools, a spokesman from the Department of Labor said quite frankly that he and his colleagues had found both labor and management much more willing to take on new responsibilities and to make changes than the school systems. He said that in many instances there was no choice but to work with the unions and employers rather than with the school system if anything was to be done inside of 20 years, or perhaps at all. I don't think this comment did any good; it was taken in partisan spirit and angered the good people of the city. But the lesson is there: if the schools can't do it, some other agency will. There are right now Department of Labor courses starting up over the country in villages and cities. For example, in the small Maine resort village where I was this summer, the Office of Manpower and Automation is financing a school to train 30 young men in shipbuilding. This is a local industry which is short of workers. There is unemployment in the area and the shipyard owners have agreed to staff the school and to employ its graduates.

Sheldon's moderate projections suggest a decade of unbelievable pressure for improvement in quality, for extension of services, for greater integration of the school system with our economic system. The premium in education during the coming years will be upon people who can innovate, who like change, development, and conflict. If our present schools of education are unable to supply such people in time, they will come in from other fields, for education is acquiring the glamour of a fast-moving field rewarding to creative ingenuity.

In his response to "America's Adults in the Sixties," Haygood is concerned with the limitations, applications, and implications of demographic statistics. The limitations, according to the author, are based on its magnitude—it is gross rather than sensitive. Furthermore it is not permanent. Its major use depends on the collection and analysis of trends and details for a particular audience. Finally, he implies the demographer could be of more help if the adult educator provided him with a conceptual framework to be used as a guide for collecting data that would be relevant.

Kenneth Haygood is a Staff Associate, Center for the Study of Liberal Education for Adults.

<u>Kenneth Haygood</u>

As an adult educator I am pleased that Sheldon has chosen to apply his talents to a description of the adult population of today and to speculations about the future.

Unfortunately, however, the adult educator is not always able to apply the findings of demographic data with quite the same directness of purpose of some other professional groups.

For some people, a population projection is almost as happy and profitable an occasion as a stock split or extra dividend notice. And the demographer, like the Roman courier bearing good news, often profits as he bears the glad tidings.

The sad fact is that even the startling data about our population boom is not, in and of itself, a sure-fire guide to the adult educator. So what good is the demographer to the adult educator <u>as a person who prescribes the kinds of educational programs to be developed</u>? The answer, of course, is no good at all. He cannot—nor does he want to, I am sure—provide the adult educator with the answer to the question, "What shall be taught to whom?"

Finding the answer to that question is the responsibility of the adult educator and he alone must carry the weight of that responsibility. He may have the help of the demographer and others to assist him in his decision-making but he, as an individual, responsible to his students, his faculty, his institution, his society, and to himself, must make the final decision.

In order to make his educational decisions the adult educator needs to bring into play three intellectual processes, the first of which involves the demographer. These are:

158

1. The collection and analysis of data.
2. The development of conceptual frameworks.
3. The application of knowledge derived from practical experience.

Although I don't intend to discuss all three of these points in detail I have mentioned them in order to stress the idea that each is a part of an interrelated process of decision-making in which the adult educator must engage.

The first of these processes, the collection and analysis of data, refers to the adult educator's attempt to understand the precise nature of the context in which he hopes to develop educational activities. It is in this activity that the demographer can be of greatest help to the adult educator, in one of two ways: by providing general information on population trends and changes that enable the adult educator to explore new areas for programming, or to withdraw from others; by providing detailed analyses of specific aspects of a problem which enables the adult educator to make refined judgments about the nature of his audience.

Let us now look at specific examples in Sheldon's paper to see how demographic data helps in understanding trends and changes that may affect the work of the adult educator.

Within the overall growth of the population Sheldon notes some variations in the distribution of the population by ages. Most notable is the rapidly increasing proportion of women over 55, and especially over 65. While he points out that the increase is not cataclysmic the adult educator might well take note of this growing pool of unoccupied women, especially since many of the women, I suspect, are financially able to afford programs of adult education. This example, then, suggests—and only suggests—a possible area of program development. Although serving this particular audience is not a new idea the work of the demographer gives the adult educator increased confidence in his belief that this audience will continue to grow in numbers and importance in the foreseeable future.

The data Sheldon presents on population movements is much more complex and intriguing. It reveals broad currents of migration—heavy in-migration to the West and out-migration from the North and Central Region, for example. Couple this fact with the known preferences of middle and upper class groups for communities with rich educational facili-

ties and the adult teacher in the West can predict an increasing demand
for his services by the traditional audience for liberally and professionally oriented programs. Individual communities in the West that are interested in attracting well-educated, high-income, professionally oriented
in-migrants might do well to concentrate on the development of high quality adult education activities which are held in the local community.

A look at Sheldon's data on central cities and suburbs suggests a
similar clumping of the adult educator's prime audience in the suburbs
and because we already know that the "flight to the suburbs" is by a predominantly white population it becomes increasingly clear that the adult
educator must alter his thinking about program development. For example, the primary locus of "traditional" programming will continually
shift from the central city to the suburbs. In the city the adult educator
will be called upon to not only continue his traditional programs but also
to come up with new programs to meet quite different needs of a predominantly Negro population which is characterized by a disadvantaged economic and educational background but which will be making rapid progress as new avenues of access to the resources of society are opened up.
This challenge to the adult educator is as clear and demanding as was
the challenge in the first three decades of this century when the wave of
immigrants came to this country. However, the task of serving the needs
of the non-white central city resident is infinitely more difficult and will
strain every resource of the adult educator.

These examples suffice, I hope, to point up the general value of the
type of data Sheldon has presented and the thoughtful reader of his paper
can find useful information on nearly every page. Let me now comment
on some of the problems the adult educator may have in using data of
this type.

First, a demographer reports his findings in terms of the magnitude
of population characteristics. But magnitudes can be deceptive when put
in the frame of reference of an individual adult educator's program. The
heady data on the growth of the population may give him the feeling that
an audience for his programs is assured but the matter of size of a potential audience is usually not a critical question for adult educators. His
problem has usually been in reaching and motivating people to attend his
programs and this often does not require a huge pool of people. For example, I once had to cancel a program on understanding the gifted child when

it was offered to the residents of the Chicago Metropolitan Region because of insufficient registrations. I then placed it in one community exclusively for the residents of that community and the program was oversubscribed. So the magnitude of the population must be carefully interpreted by the adult educator.

Second, differences in demographic data are often not sensitive enough to reveal significant factors of interest to the adult educator. Data on rural-urban differences are so gross that one has difficulty in planning specific programs for audiences that are meant to fall in one or the other category. This problem is becoming even more confused as the suburban areas grow for, as Sheldon readily admits in his paper, the term "suburb" is poorly defined. Thus, the grossness of the categories masks the important differences in the qualities of the individuals. This problem can only be overcome by working with the demographer and other social scientists in sensitive investigations of sub-samples of the national population.

Third, an adult educator can be misled by an assumption of permanence as a quality of the data. He may feel that the data, so neatly arranged and codified, is a reflection of reality. In fact, as Sheldon points out, much of the data is transitory—out of date by the time it is printed. Thus, an uncritical adult educator can be easily led astray in the use of census data.

If demographic data is of limited although important use in its unrefined form, as I have been suggesting, then we ought to take a look at the way the data can be refined in order to be of specific help.

The only way to determine what data is to be collected and what is to be ignored is to develop a "conceptual framework" or "viewpoint"— the second intellectual process employed by the adult educator as he makes educational decisions. When the adult educator has such a framework he can then begin to zero in on his target and decide what kind of data he needs. Let us now take an example and see how this works in practice.

Havighurst, in his paper for this meeting provides us with a very useful conceptual framework, one of many that can be used. He describes the social roles of the adult as a "complex of behavior appropriate to a given position in social life, defined by the expectations of society and of the individual." He further suggests that "educational programs can be conceived to help people improve their performance of these roles."

The use of this concept enables one to focus his thinking about adults so that he can then turn to the demographer for specific information about adult social roles. For example, when we take the first role mentioned by Havighurst, "worker," we are immediately interested in the answers to these questions, among others: How many workers are there? What kinds of work do they do? How are they distributed in the population? What changes have been taking place in the labor force? What do projections into the future seem to indicate? How are these data related to other data, such as population movements, changes in income levels, increase in education?

Although the answers to many of these questions would require more refined treatment of the data than was requested of Sheldon for this seminar we can find some interesting leads in his paper. Sheldon states that there has been a downward trend in the proportion of men participating in the labor force, interrupted only briefly during the peak years of World War II, probably due to technological changes. Among women, the labor force participation shows an appreciable increase, but with two peaks— one at 20 to 24 and the other in the middle years. Again, this participation rate seems to be a part of a long-term trend. He further points out that women seem to have a more tenuous connection with the labor force and suggests that there is competition for a woman's time between employment and her family responsibilities. Putting this in Havighurst's terms there is then solid evidence of a "conflict in social roles" which many women must face. Armed with this kind of specific knowledge derived from the work of the demographer and working with the construct of a useful concept about adults the educator can then develop sensitive programs to meet very specific needs. And, if the adult educator works in areas where the demographer has projected an increasing need for a particular type of program the educator can be assured that his work may bear fruit for many years rather than simply being a "one-shot" program.

These examples are intended to show that if the adult educator goes to the demographer with a specific educational target in mind the demographer can begin to collect the refined data needed for careful program development. But until the educator accepts the burden for defining his particular needs and works cooperatively with the demographer we can

162

expect only limited and general assistance. While the burden of developing a cooperative relationship with the demographer may be primarily on the back of the adult educator it is reasonable to expect that the demographer will respond to adult education's needs by developing studies and classifications of data more suited to our needs.

With the rapid changes in population taking place and the increasing need for highly specialized educational experiences for adults the development of demographic research in adult education is a matter of highest priority.

* * *

Responding to the "Adult Uses of Education," the author suggests implications that may be drawn from Johnstone's findings. He believes special attention must be paid to the rhythm of education, especially for women, and to finding ways to increase the holding power of adult education. The Johnstone data also inspired him to comment on three mischievous notions about education: (1) schooling is the same as education; (2) extension courses are second rate; and (3) summer school is for those with low academic standards.

Robert H. Beck is a philosopher of education from the University of Minnesota.

Robert H. Beck

The design of Johnstone's study included an area probability sample of over 13,000 households, 90 per cent of whom actually were subject to screening interviews (see his Table 1). This screening produced almost 24,000 adults. Two thousand, eight hundred and forty-five, hour-long interviews were held with members of these households.

It is impossible to comment on the design of Johnstone's paper without reference to the complete NORC report. It goes without saying that Johnstone's readers will wish to know precisely what characterization of social class he has employed. If, as would seem to be true, Johnstone has limited himself to "objective" characteristics such as income, type of employment, year of last schooling attended by self and parents, further research should be conducted on the adult education potentiality within the lower class. This is suggested simply because we know that many people typed as lower-class by income et cetera, may be middle-class in their ambitions and values. This matter of "identification," of self-perception, and self-anchoring, as Cantril[1] puts it, is significant.

1. Cantril, Hadley. "A Study in Aspirations," Scientific American, 208 (No. 2), 41-45, February, 1963.

Some Principal Findings

(1) One of the most heartening and impressive findings in Johnstone's study is the degree of adult participation in continuing education, a phrase I prefer to adult education simply because continuing education hints that education can be continuous throughout adult life, if we learn how to sustain adult interest. Although Johnstone draws attention to weaknesses in both the drawing and holding power of contemporary adult or continuing education, the future of continuing education looks bright indeed.

The fact that Johnstone found interests shifting with age, with the degree of family responsibility, and so forth, makes it essential that adult education be even more flexible, much more flexible and opportunistic, than conventional schooling. Adult education, if poised to change, can be more adventurous, more imaginative, than any other form of education.

I should like to move from Johnstone's specific findings to an issue of general import in adult education, the rhythm of education. Johnstone prompts the discussion by suggesting some personal characteristics of those who are potential adult education participants. Put quickly, these men and women are interested in learning. If this is true, we can say once again that those teaching in pre-adult education must do better in capitalizing on motives and in both awakening interest in learning and sustaining that interest. We continue to hide behind compulsory attendance laws and add the threat of unemployment of the drop-out.

Perhaps the more serious failure is in remaining captive of historical accidents such as having a lower, middle (in this country called Junior High) and higher education, each with standard spans of years. Schooling is Procrustean. We will have to adjust to part-time schooling even for boys and girls of fifteen. It goes without saying that the adult interest in independent study ought to lead us away from the model of daily classroom instruction by the teacher; lecture by professors and recitation by students.

Dr. Johnstone found that 7.9% of adults involved in organized educational pursuits over a one-year period studied on their own and 15% had studied on a part-time basis. I should like to suggest that this percentage can be increased, if another academic habit can be broken. There is nothing original in suggesting that students, even in the lower schools, need not always be sitting in classes being talked or lectured at. Today

164

the phrase "independent study" is all the thing. Independent study assumes that listening and watching a blackboard or television screen is not the prime manner of being instructed. Pari passu teaching is altered by independent study; it becomes more guidance and less pouring on. Individual differences are given more scope. Table 3 in Johnstone's study shows that 44% of courses were taken outside classrooms. Table 4 reveals that only one-third were taken in schools. Other agencies and institutions are promoting adult education; their efforts need to be studied and coordinated. Adult education has been a good deal less hide-bound and can help the rest of us catch up in our instructional techniques. The reciprocal of our advance will be more students willing to go on with instruction when they are past the usual age of students or after their formal schooling has been interrupted.

Incidentally, it is high time that Americans adopted into American-English the habit other nationals have of distinguishing schooling from education. We make the two identical and think, therefore, that sturdy education ends with a diploma. There are several of these termini, with the most advanced being the Ph.D. There ought to be more flexibility.

It must become possible to easily break one's formal schooling at more points than at the age of sixteen or with graduation from high school or junior college or college or with an MA. These arbitrary points are historical accidents. They are disfunctional. And the patterns of school experiences are disfunctional because too seldom conceived for individuals. Why should there be a college-preparatory course of study rather than courses in mathematics, literature, languages, and so on for Mr. or Miss X, Y, and Z? Admittedly we are doing better with individuating programs; we have more and more guidance-counseling in our high schools and, lately, in our colleges. But the rhythm of schooling, its sequences and breaks have not been produced by experimentation. Fruitful research could be done on the subject.

It is mischievious to tell a young lady, "you must complete any pre-professional study in four years of college." Many marry before passing on to professional schools. They are out of schools a decade or more and feel quite unable to attempt entering a medical school, for example, because their pre-professional study now is too old. Yet Johnstone finds women anxious to take up adult education after the age of 40 (Table 10). Would it be impossible to frame a program of undergraduate studies for women that would concentrate on acquisition of skills and information least likely to become obsolescent? Logical and statistical analysis, methods of establishing inferences, ability to write and speak, literature, history, foreign languages all seem stable. The discipline of political science may be altered by becoming more a study of political behavior but the modern tools for studying human behavior are not likely to alter radically in a decade or two. Let educators look for the more enduring studies, which is what Plato urged, if I am not mistaken.

The Minnesota Plan for Women's Continuing Education[2] provides interesting data to compare with that reported by Johnstone.[3] There is information on some 900 women who have applied to participate in the program. Two-thirds of the applicants fell into the age range 28-47. Johnstone has 25 per cent of women who studied any subject younger than 35 and 21 per cent 35-54 years of age. The Minnesota Plan attracted relatively few women less than 28 and no more older than 47.

Johnstone does not report the number of children had by the mothers canvassed in his study. In the Minnesota Plan five of every seven women applying had from two to four children. Two of every seven had three children and one of seven had four children.

The Minnesota sample is preempted by upper-middle class women, some cue to that fact being that three out of each seven had had some college and an equal number were college graduates. One out of seven had gone beyond college. Four of every seven were married to men in managerial or professional jobs.

Johnstone's conclusion that education feeds upon itself is borne out by the Minnesota experience. Two-and-a-half of every seven applicants had had some form of "informal" education within four years of their application.

As reasons for enrolling in the program applicant women more than half of the time gave "self-enrichment" as a reason. This bears out Johnstone (Table 12). The upper-social classes, as Johnstone notes, have fewer

---

2. Virginia Senders, "The Minnesota Plan for Women's Continuing Education: A Progress Report," Unfinished Business: Continuing Education for Women. The Commission on the Education of Women of the American Council on Education, pp. 10-18, 1962.

3. "Newsletter," The Minnesota Plan for the Continuing Education of Women, University of Minnesota, February, 1963.

vocational interests. But one of the purposes generating the Minnesota Plan was to "return to the manpower pool (whether paid or unpaid) intelligent, educated women whose abilities would otherwise be unused or underused during their mature years."[4] When the applicants were asked to indicate their interests self-enrichment[5] was checked most often (416 times) with "undergraduate degree within five years" (286 times), "training in new field of specialization" (254 times), graduate degree (208 times), "increased professional competence" (195 times) next in line. "Retraining in field of earlier specialization" was checked only 105 times, which would suggest that we may not be wise to gear education of adult women to refreshing their skills. Women wish new fields to conquer.

Esther Raushenbush[6] reminds all interested in continuing education that women have had the least imaginative model of higher education and, I would suggest, secondary education as well. This is not the place, perhaps, to reflect upon the high school instruction for girls but it almost never involves sex education, family planning, or a realistic study of the responsibilities incurred by marriage. Colleges for women simply duplicated those for men, their purpose, Miss Raushenbush feeling, being nothing more than to see whether women could sustain the same sort of college education as was given men. It takes no seer to prophesy that more intelligent planning of the education of women must be made.

I should like to suggest that this inquiry into adult education has spotted at least three notions now widely touted but mischievious for all their popularity. One is that education is the same as schooling. A sec-one is an idol of the academy: that Extension courses are necessarily second-rate[7] and that summer school is only for those whose academic standards are low. Presumably Extension courses are at a discount because laboratory and library may not be available or because students

---

4. "The Minnesota Plan To Sustain Learning," Quarterly, Carnegie Corporation of New York, X, No. 4, October, 1962, p. 2.

5. "Newsletter," op. cit.

6. Raushenbush, Esther, Unfinished Business: Continuing Education for Women. The Commission on the Education of Women of the American Council on Education, 1962.

7. Conant, James B., The Education of American Teachers. New York: McGraw-Hill Book Company, Inc., 1963, Chap. 9.

study after a full day of work. I know of no empirical study of the attainment of students taking Extension courses and think that in the absence of discouraging information the discounting of Extension courses, by such scholars as Conant, is to be viewed as prejudice. So too with summer school which usually is criticized for being too short. The number of class hours and hours of preparation by student and professor may be the same as quarter courses in the Fall, Winter, and Spring, but few critics trouble to count such things.

Johnstone tells that only 2.3 per cent of adults involved in organized educational pursuits over a one-year period were "full-time students." Twenty-odd per cent were active other than as full-time students. Although schooling past high school is likely to become even more the usual thing than it now is, it is doubtful that even a thirty-hour week will permit much of an increase in full-time adult education. The design, staffing, and resources of part-time study must be enhanced.

Elizabeth Cless, presently the Director of the Minnesota Plan for Women's Continuing Education, assured me—and I submit the proposition to you for critique—that the traditional view of Extension study needs reconstruction in the direction of substituting the concept of part-time education. Johnstone learned (Table 1) that only 2.3 per cent of his sample had been full-time students. Mrs. Cless would have colleges and universities modify their admission policies, alter their incidental fee charges, and other details, to encourage students who wish to study part-time. I suggest that this thought merits close study, though its implementation would call for radical revision of Extension work. Nor am I speaking of a negligible fraction of adult education. In Johnstone's survey (Table 4) 21 per cent attended courses at colleges and universities. Were these institutions to attempt increasing the enrollment of part-time students, it would be a fair guess that this fraction would increase. After all there is prestige attached to college or university attendance and the atmosphere of the campus is attractive.

It would seem that adult education has not enjoyed a greater holding power than schooling in general. Johnstone reports that the typical case was active just once or twice. Apparently the experience was not altogether rewarding even though it had been freely entered upon—only 26 per cent of all courses were taken for credit toward some degree. This is a challenge to teachers of adults because the motivation was high—

most courses elected being vocational or recreational. Tempering this rather negative interpretation is the fact that the largest share of courses were vocational (34 per cent) and may be thought largely terminal. That is, a man takes a course or two to learn a particular skill. Having learned it he may cease to take courses unless there are courses available that take him to a higher level in that skill. I do not know whether the prevailing pattern of vocational courses tends not to carry the level of skill beyond a "beginner" or intermediate quality. If this were the case leaders in adult education should explore the possibility of offering advanced work. The character of interest appears to be utilitarian and might be exploited by a higher level of course. Once that higher level is reached it may be that the student could be drawn into a consideration of some topics associated with his specialty. This is one manner of approaching a general education and I think a more promising one than expecting a general education to be accomplished by enrolling students in a variety of introductory courses.

Johnstone mentions that one's degree of optimism about the future, influence of other people, and status changes in one's life, affect an interest in adult education. The degree of optimism can best be measured by such an instrument as Conant's self-anchoring scale. I have no suggestion on how optimism can be increased. Certainly elementary and high school teachers can help their colleagues in adult education by making education attractive. On the third point, change in status, I am sure life in the future will be no less changeful. If horizontal mobility increases an interest in learning, that interest will not decrease because of less movement of people in the next twenty years.

To make a last and quite minor suggestion, those who dropped out of school before graduating from high school often were poor readers. Adult education courses that involve a good deal of reading, and most do, will not succeed in attracting those who did not make it through high school or who barely did so. Just as high schools and upper-elementary grades must find reading materials whose content holds the interest of older students at the time as the vocabulary level is low, men and women in adult education must do this same thing for adults and it will not be easy. Research and extended field trial of materials are called for.